DAMAYANTI

She who spurned the gods...
all for love of Nal

Shivdutt Sharma

YogiImpressions®

DAMAYANTI
First published in India in 2017 by
Yogi Impressions Books Pvt. Ltd.
1711, Centre 1, World Trade Centre,
Cuffe Parade, Mumbai 400 005, India.
Website: www.yogiimpressions.com

First Edition, August 2017

Front Cover Illustration: Vijay Ugale
Inside Cover Illustration: Girish Jathar

Disclaimer: This is a work of fiction. While it remains true to the main story of Nal and Damayanti narrated in the Vana Parva of the Mahabharata epic, certain fictional characters have been introduced for interest and dramatic impact. All effort has been taken to represent certain facts as accurately as they have been gathered from various sources. Any oversights or errors are genuinely regretted.

ISBN 978-93-82742-55-5

Printed at: Repro India Ltd., Mumbai

Prologue

While the Pandava brothers were living in exile in the Kamyaka forest along the banks of the Saraswati river, on the western boundary of the Kuru kingdom, the revered sage Vrihadaswa honoured them with a visit. Beholding the illustrious Rishi, Yudhishtra, the eldest of the Pandava brothers, accorded him great respect and a gracious welcome by presenting the *Madhuparka* – a refreshing offering made of honey, curd and ghee. He then bewailed his lament to the sage:

'O holy one, invited by the cunning Kauravas to a game of dice, I have been stripped of all my wealth and kingdom through a rigged game. Though myself an adept at dice, I did not suspect they would resort to any trickery or deceit. Thus having lost all in the gamble, including my wife Draupadi, we have all been sent into exile for 13 years.'

Vrihadaswa clucked his tongue sympathetically.

Yudhishtra continued his lament. 'Recollecting that fateful day, I am extremely distressed that due to my addiction to gambling, I have brought misfortune to my family. I wonder if there has ever been any other king on this earth who has suffered greater misfortune than me. I doubt if there has been any man more wretched than I am.'

Vrihadaswa sighed and consoled him by saying, 'Take heart, noble son of Pandu. I will relate the story of one such King who suffered even greater misfortune than you. There was the celebrated King Nal of the Nishadhas who was similarly defeated by his younger brother in a game of dice and banished, along with his wife and two children, from his kingdom. You on the other hand, have your four heroic brothers, and your wife, to support you in this most grievous hour. Therefore, it does not suit you to grieve and lament the fate you have brought upon yourself.'

Yudhishtra, with an air of dejection, pleaded with the sage, 'I am most anxious to hear in detail, the story of King Nal, and how he overcame his predicament.'

Vrihadaswa then said, 'Gather your brothers and your wife around you, so you can all listen to the inspiring tale of Nal and Damayanti...'

Map of
Central India
in the time of
Mahabharata –
around 3500 BCE.

The Flight of the Swans
Manasarovar – Giriprastha – Kundinapuri

Depicted in this map are the regions of Vidarbha, Nishadha, Ayodhya (Mithila), Sukmati (Chedi) in which the story of Nal and Damayanti takes place.

Map not to scale

Part 1

Messengers Of Love

Chapter 1

The Mortal Who Rivalled The Gods

'Brilliant as Surya... fair as Chandra...
handsome as the Ashvins... desirable as Kama...
glorious as Indra'

Rishis and sages praised his noble character, learning and valour...

Chitrakars and shilpakars competed to capture his godlike appearance...

Sutradhars and bards outdid one another in praise of his skills as a charioteer...

He was the envy of princes and warriors in kingdoms far and wide...

And, he was the fantasy and the dream of every woman.

He was Nal.

The extraordinarily handsome and valiant prince of Nishadha.

The heir apparent of King Virasena.

With its capital city at Giriprastha[1], the prosperous Nishadha kingdom of Virasena lay north of the Vindhya mountain range that separated it from the kingdom of Vidarbha. Linked by busy trade routes that connected it to the kingdoms of nearby Chedi, Dasarna, Kosala, Matsya, Magadha, as well as with that of Vidarbha – it thrived on its rich mineral wealth of semi-

[1] According to the Mahabharata (Book 3 – 324, 12), the capital of the Nishadhas was Giriprastha, which most likely is the present-day Gwalior in Madhya Pradesh.

precious stones, such as lapis lazuli that were mined from the Nila mountain, and the opals from the Sweta mountain, while the metals were mined from the Sringavat mountains nearby. The land owed its fertile soil and greening to the largesse of the Pyoshini River. Teeming with fish and marine life, it flowed from the Vindhyas through the Nishadha kingdom and then, upon entering from the northern point of the wild, dense and dreaded Dandaka forest, it ran to flow into the ocean.

Walking along the riverbank with his childhood friend Rudra, the young prince was idly casting stones when a palace guard rode up to them. Saluting briskly, he stuttered, 'Ra-Ra-Rajkumar… Her Highness, your mother, requires your presence in the Lotus Hall.'

'Catch your breath, Purshottam… what's the rush? I hope it's not another painter who has come to paint my portrait!' sighed Nal.

'Well, that's the price you have to pay for your good looks!' ribbed Rudra. 'By the way, how many portraits are there adorning the hallways of the palace? At last count, there were twenty-two I think. Oh-oh… I get it. You will be turning a year older in a few days from now, so I think your mother wants to commemorate your birthday by having a new portrait painted.'

'What on earth is she going to do with this collection, I can't fathom!' said Nal, throwing up his hands.

'Probably get a few copies made of the latest one to send out to fathers of prospective young girls of marriageable age,' chortled Rudra.

'Ha-ha, you are always thinking of girls!'

'Well… I wish they would start thinking of me for a change, instead of mooning and swooning over you! I don't look half-bad you know, Nal!'

'Oh, not at all! You just remind me of the backside of a bull!' teased Nal. 'Hey-hey… stop, stop…' he laughed as Rudra playfully pounded him with his balled-up fists. 'Okay, okay. I take that back… your face looks like the dark night of amavasya!'

'Come on… race you back to the palace,' shouted Rudra as he sprinted away gaining a headstart over Nal and laughing at his own cleverness.

'You rascal,' Nal shook his fist and ran after him. Kicking out his left foot, he tackled Rudra who tripped and stumbled on the path while Nal jeered and raced ahead.

Huffing and puffing, the two friends arrived at the palace and ran down the corridors towards the Lotus Hall.

'Ah-ha, there you are! Son, come and look at the portrait of this lovely princess which Chitrakar Visheshwara has brought,' the Queen Mother gestured towards a painting that rested on a stand and was draped over with fine muslin.

'Oh, Mother… you called me just for this!' moaned Nal clutching his hair. *She will be just another pretty face of some kingdom or the other.* Rudra clapped a hand to his mouth and tried to smother the snigger that was rising in him.

'At least take a look, Nal,' the Queen Mother said gently. Pushkar, her younger son added his plea to hers: 'Yes, brother… please do! If you don't get married first, my turn will never come!'

'Besides, Visheshwara is famous for his art of capturing the very likeness of his subjects and has travelled many miles from Madra to bring her portrait to us,' said his mother. Then she added the clincher, 'and as you well know, the princesses of Madra are famed for their beauty!'

Rudra made sounds of clearing his throat, 'Your Highness… if I my say something…'

'Of course, son… you are as dear to me as Nal,' Queen Vasumati encouraged him.

'Nal has been raving, quite madly if I may say so, about a damsel who has been appearing in his dreams…'

'What utter rubbish!' exclaimed a flustered, blushing Nal. 'Mother, no such thing… don't listen to this mad fellow, he is lying…'

Visheshwara came forward and bowing low, suggested, 'Your Highness, if the young Prince can describe the fair maiden of his dreams, perhaps I could paint a picture of her likeness…'

The Queen Mother clapped her hands, delighted with this. 'Yes, of course… what a brilliant idea! Our Nal is quite the poet and I am sure he will wax lyrical over this dream girl,' she laughed.

'Mother!' Nal blushed several shades deeper. 'Honestly… you people are just too much!'

'I will hear no more of it, Nal!'

Then turning to Visheshwara, she said: 'Will you please paint a portrait of this girl while my son describes her to you?'

The painter stroked his beard thoughtfully and mused, 'It may take a while but I shall do all that is within my talents to capture her likeness, Your Highness.'

'You are a traitor, Rudra!' groaned Nal when they were alone. 'You blabbered what I told you in confidence about my dreams.'

'Rubbish, I just proved what a good friend I am! At least now we will see who has been haunting you in your dreams these past nights, and soon we will know if she is just a figment of your imagination or whether such a maiden really exists!'

Chapter 2

THE PAINTER OF DREAMS

Nal entered his private chambers together with Rudra to see Visheshwara arranging the tools of his craft, his pens, brushes, dyes and paints, alongside an easel on which stood a cured square of the finest bark of the eucalyptus tree. A fragrant, bluish haze arose from copper incense burners placed on wrought iron tripods. Screened by a gauzy veil of curtains, musicians struck the soft, opening notes of a raga as nubile handmaidens offered goblets of scented and watered wine.

Raising his goblet in a toast, Rudra declared, 'Here's to the weaver of dreams… may success be bestowed on this experiment.'

'Hear, hear… I raise my toast to that,' echoed Visheshwara. 'Come, Prince, drink to that… and may the vision of beauty part the veils of mist of your subconscious mind and reappear. My art will strive to interpret and capture the image of the face and form whose every feature you will describe.'

'Come recline on your couch. Close your eyes and allow the musical strains of the *veena* lull you into a dream-like trance,' intoned Visheshwara who had earlier administered a mild opiate in the drink to the young man. 'She who haunts your dreams will reveal herself. As you call out to her from the depths of your heart, she is bound come…'

As Nal drifted into a slumber, his breathing slowed down and became deeper. His eyelids felt heavy as he gradually began to murmur …

'Deep in the inner recesses of my slumbering mind
She flashes like a brilliant bolt of lightning
Her raven locks framing a face lovely as the moon
That with its dazzling beauty would a mortal blind...'

Visheshwara first picked up his sharp-nibbed pen made of bamboo reed and dipped it in the indigo dye. With deft strokes he drew the outlines of a face, around which he sketched a flash of lightning in a midnight blue sky that he quickly painted on a cloth. 'Go on Prince, tell me more,' he cajoled.

'Like two new moons rising above long-lashed eyes
Are brows as smoothly curved as Kamadev's bow
A diamond sparkles on her pert, parrot-beaked nose
Two dimples appear in rounded cheeks as she smiles...'

'A vision of ethereal beauty… perhaps she is some beauteous apsara from Indra's swargalok,' sighed Visheshwara. Tell me more…'

'Her chin is finely chiselled and resolutely set
She has a graceful arch to her swan-like neck
Her gaze penetrates the depths of my soul
An inner calm and confident poise she reflects.'

Visheshwara's hand deftly mixed a colour palette of pastel and vivid hues and with the rapid strokes of his squirrel-hair brushes, he began colouring the face that was taking shape on the cured, smoothened and thin sheet of bark.

'That tiny mole auspiciously dotting the ajna chakra at its centre
Would drive a god, leave alone any man, insane with desire
Her bosom in its full blossom of youth heaves with every breath
As her slender, girdled waist sways from side to side on curved hips.'

Adding a few finishing strokes to the painting, Visheshwara put aside his pens and brushes and wiped his hands on a piece of cloth. More or less satisfied with the painting, he walked towards the reclining form of Nal and putting a gentle hand on his shoulder shook him out of his reverie.

'Wake up Prince and tell me, if this is the face that appears in your dreams? Is this the face that has you mesmerised and that you long to see?'

Nal's eyes fluttered open and rising languorously from the couch, he walked slowly towards the face that was drawing him hypnotically towards itself. He heard Rudra exclaim, 'By Rudra! She appears to be an apsara, and the most beautiful one at that, of Indra's court!'

It was a fair likeness. *Yes*, Nal thought to himself, rubbing his eyes to clear his vision. The tiny mole was in the right place... the two dark pools of her eyes, by some trick of the painter's art, seem to follow his gaze no matter from which angle he viewed the painting.

'Raj Mata Vasumati Devi padhaar rahi hain...' announced the guard posted outside Nal's chambers as his staff thumped the floor to signal her arrival.

'So, Visheshwaraji, has the dream girl materialised from my son's dreams?' she asked with a smile. 'Ah-h... so this is her!' she added, going up to the painting. 'By any chance, do you know who she is?'

Visheshwara bowed in greeting. 'I could hazard a guess Rajmata, although my painting does not do her full justice. I have not seen her myself but from all the descriptions that I have heard from poets, bards and other chitrakars in the course of my travels... she could be the Princess of Vidarbha.'

'Damayanti?' the Queen Mother said with a note of mild surprise. 'The daughter of King Bhima?'

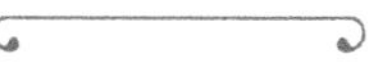

Chapter 3

SHE WHO WALKS IN BEAUTY

A pearl among maidens... without rival or peer...
In the heavens above, or the earth below...
Her incandescent beauty dazzles immortals and mortals...
Like lightning flashing in the midst of dark clouds.

Sounds of laughter rippled through the hallways of the palace as a group of giggly girls played *lukka-chhuppi*, their favourite game of hide-n-seek. Videhi, who was the one to be blind-folded this time, ran this way and that whenever her ears pricked up to the tinkling of anklets, or hushed whispers behind the columns. Damayanti sneaked up behind Videhi and gave her a playful pinch.

The princess of Vidarbha, Damayanti, in her sixteenth summer, was blossoming into a beautiful maiden. Along with her three brothers Dama, Danta and Damana, she had been born as the result of a boon given by the Rishi Damana to King Bhima and his Queen who, for long, had been childless. Apart from lavishing their love on her, they had seen to every facet of her education and learning and in the process of raising a confident, caring and conscious child, had the wisest of sages attend to moulding her character and personality. Always surrounded by the prettiest of handmaidens, but none that matched her beauty, Damayanti bloomed like a rose in the fabled gardens of the royal palace at Kundina[1].

Most people who had the occasion to be in her presence

[1] Kundinapuri, which was its full name, was shortened to Kundina by its citizens.

could not see beyond her beauty. They seemed blinded to what lay behind her lovely face and graceful form. Outwardly compliant, she was an intelligent girl with a mind of her own; one who had the courage of her convictions. A truly romantic heart beat in her young bosom, but beneath all that softness lurked a firm, resolute and fearless will. If she set her mind on a course of action, she left no stone unturned to see it to its successful conclusion. This aspect of her personality, of which she herself was perhaps quite oblivious, had been keenly observed by Chitra, her closest companion and confidante.

Videhi let out a delighted scream as she grabbed the arm of one of the girls who had passed within an inch of her. Ripping off her blindfold, she shrieked, 'Caught one of you at last! Now you will see what it is like to run blindly into pillars and flower beds once I tie this piece of cloth across your eyes!'

Chitra ran up to them. 'Girls! Enough of running around! Let's take a break and rest a while. Come, the maids have laid out delightful refreshments for us under the awning of Sakhiyon ki Baithak.'

'Yes, let's all gather there,' said Rukmini, a plump young girl, who was delicately mopping the sweat of her brow with the edge of her dupatta. 'I am famished after all the running around. Why on earth Damayanti chooses this hour in the afternoon to play hide and seek is beyond me!'

'It's all for your own good, Rukmini,' answered Damayanti coming up to them. 'Isn't she looking much trimmer than when she first joined our inner circle?'

'Dushyant, that young palace guard, certainly thinks so,' teased Malini. 'I have seen him making eyes at her for some time now. Isn't that so, Rukmini?' she asked, which made the young girl blush to the roots of her hair.

'Ah-hhh… when will some handsome young Prince come my way…' sighed Damayanti.

'The princes of this land are probably scared to come anywhere near you, because of your three strapping brothers!' mocked Chitra. 'Especially Danta, that middle brother of yours!

His looks and bearing are so stern that they would scare the living daylights out of any mortal!'

'Huh!' scoffed Damayanti. 'I don't want just any mortal man. I want the handsomest one in all this land.'

'What about Prince Debadatta of Vanga?' piped up Videhi.

'Ha! Him?' exclaimed Rukmini. 'I hear he is already going bald and is also pretty short!'

'Okay, not him then! How about Prince Kaushal of Magadha?' asked another of the girls.

'Well... I hear he is tall and good-looking,.. and very skilled with the sword, but...' ventured Kumudini.

'But what?' queried Chitra.

'Hmmm... I hear he sta-ta-stammers... takes forever to string a few words together!'

At this, all of them let out peals of laughter.

'What about Matsya? That's nearby and I have heard they have a couple of eligible princes.'

'Oh, no! Forget that stretch of desert. Everyone wilts there... especially the youth of pretty maidens like us,' lamented another.

A gust of cool breeze floated in the air and ruffled the curls that were cascading down Damayanti's head. It swept aside a curl from her ear and whispered the words, *Nal... Nal... Prince of Nishadha.*

She turned to see who had whispered that name into her ear but all her friends were busy talking among themselves. A smile hovered on her lips. *Am I hallucinating... who whispered that name in my ear?* she wondered, twirling the curl around her finger.

Suddenly, the high-pitched voice of Videhi broke from the girls gathered around her. 'I know... I know... how could we forget! Girls... how about Prince Nal? I have heard there is none more handsome ... they even say the gods are jealous of him!'

Damayanti was jolted out of her reverie. *Was this sheer coincidence?* Flustered, she asked, 'But has anyone of you seen Prince Nal? Rumours often turn out to be highly coloured and exaggerated, especially when they are praising the beauty or some virtue of a person.'

The girls looked askance at each other. Few of them had ever stepped beyond the walls of the palace gardens.

Chitra snapped her fingers. 'I know what… let's call that new palace maid… Bharati, who has just joined the royal kitchens as junior cook. I heard someone say that she is from Nishadha. Let's ask her and hear what she has to say, shall we?'

'Good idea!' agreed Videhi.

'I am not staying. What will my mother say if she hears I have been gossiping with the kitchen maid?' exclaimed Damayanti.

'Oh, don't be so scared Damayanti!' protested Chitra. 'All right, you can hide behind that pillar and listen to what she has to tell us.'

Bharati, the kitchen maid, came wiping her hands nervously on the sides of her long skirt.

'Come, come… don't feel shy,' Chitra said gently. 'We hear you are from the land of Nishadha?'

'Yy-e-ss… I am, my lady…'

'In what capacity were you working there?'

'I was a handmaiden to the Queen Mother, my lady.'

'Ah-ha… then you must have had many an opportunity to see Prince Nal! Tell us how he looks! Is he all that handsome as they say he is?'

Bharati blushed and lowered her head.

'Come, come… don't feel shy,' prodded Videhi.

Head still lowered, Bharati giggled. 'He is handsome, very handsome… not very tall, but very strong.'

'Tell us more about him,' Chitra persisted.

'I have only heard that he is very fond of playing the game of dice. But I have seen him drive a chariot and this I can say… no one can steer the horses the way he does. I think he whispers magic words into the ears of those horses! Oh, and there is another secret not many know about and I am not going to tell…'

'Come on, you can tell us… we promise we won't tell anyone.'

'I will lose my job if it gets out that I told you…' protested Bharati.

'We promise not to tell anyone. Now, what is that secret? Do tell!'

'Sometimes, he comes to the kitchen and observes us cooking. He asks the maharaj who is the head cook all sorts of questions… what spices he is using, how much salt he is putting, whether to use red or green chillies in a particular dish… why, at times, he even picks up the ladle to stir the broth or slices off a piece of meat to taste how well it has been done!'

'Really, is that true? Well, anyway… tell us more about his looks!' Rukmini piped up.

'Once, I had gone to fill the water in his bath… His skin is pale as moonbeams… it has a silver-like whiteness and sheen. His body is tough and muscular… oh-ohh… I almost dropped the vessel in which I was carrying the water!' blushed Bharati.

The girls guffawed with delight at this revelation of Bharati.

'Run off now, you naughty girl!' laughed Chitra, as Bharati gathered up her long skirt and ran away giggling to herself.

'You can come out now Damayanti,' said Chitra as she drew her out from behind the pillar. 'So there you have it from someone who has actually seen Prince Nal with her very own eyes. What a lucky girl to have feasted her eyes on him in the bath,' she sniggered.

'Oh, hush Chitra! Stop saying such things before these innocent girls!' Damayanti said in mock alarm. 'Some of them are far too young to hear talk of half-naked men!'

'How do you know he was half-naked, may I ask, Damayanti? Bharati never said any such thing. You, girl, are already letting your imagination run a wee bit wild,' Chitra teased.

That night, alone in her bedchamber, Damayanti tossed and turned through the night unable to get a wink of sleep. Her mind kept conjuring up imaginary images of Nal. *Is he really so good looking?* she wondered, because nothing of what she had heard so far helped create a mental picture of him.

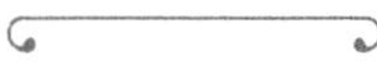

Chapter 4

A Bevy Of Swans

The day had dawned bright and sunny. Stepping down from the chariot after having given a good workout to the horses for the annual championship that was drawing near, Nal handed over the reins to the groom and instructed him to lead them to drink water from the trough. His high brow and broad chest were dripping sweat. On the spur of the moment, he impulsively jumped into the canal that ran through the palace grounds and irrigated its splendid gardens abloom in a riot of colour. After having splashed around in the cool waters, Nal was languidly floating on his back with his eyes closed when he heard a rhythmic flutter of wings and their high-pitched, quavering call as they drew close. He opened his eyes and looked up to see a bevy of swans gliding towards the canal. *But what was that glint that was causing his eyes to screw up tight as it bounced off their outstretched wings?* he wondered. Raising a hand to shield his eyes from the glinting beam, he saw the swans land gracefully on the water. Silently, so that his movement would not frighten them away, he floated towards them and was amazed to see that two of the swans among the bevy had golden wings.

Where have these golden-winged swans come from? They have never been sighted before! I must somehow capture this golden pair, Nal vowed as he tugged at the tender stems and roots of a few lotus leaves and, clutching them, swam quietly ashore. He crawled along the bank towards this golden pair and held out the leaves, tempting the swans to come closer. The golden-winged pen, the female swan, glided towards Nal's outstretched hand and stretched out its neck to peck at the leaf. As soon as it did that, Nal trapped its neck in the crook of his arm and lifted the bird onto the shore. Its male partner ruffled and flapped its wings, waddled on to the lawn and began pecking angrily at Nal's shoulder in an attempt to rescue its mate. His younger brother Pushkar, who had seen this scene from a distance, ran forward and grabbed the cob by the neck and pulled it away from Nal. Upon hearing all this commotion and the plaintive hoots of the golden swans, the startled bevy of swans flew away in their wedge formation in the sky.

'Whatever are you going to do with this pair, Nal?' asked Pushkar still grappling with the swan he had captured.

'Aren't they unbelievably beautiful, Pushkar... have you, or anyone else, ever seen a pair of golden-winged swans before in your life? They will add to the fame and glory of Nishadha and be the envy of all our neighbouring princes and kings!' remarked an evidently thrilled and delighted Nal. 'I can just imagine the look on my mother's face when she sees these rare swans! She will be overjoyed!'

'I wonder how they are to taste,' said Pushkar stroking the bird's neck. 'Let's kill one and roast it!'

Hearing this, the female swan let out a wild shriek and wailed, 'What have we poor creatures ever done for you to kill one of us?'

'Don't you know it would be a sin to kill a swan!' exclaimed the male swan. 'Haven't you studied your scriptures, Pushkar? We represent the Supreme Spirit – the Brahman-atma. We are the vehicle of the goddess of music and learning – Sri Saraswati!'

Shocked out of his wits at hearing the swans speak in a human tongue, Nal's grip slackened and the swan straightened and then gracefully withdrew its neck from his hold. Tears rolled down its eyes as it looked pleadingly at Nal. 'Please, do not kill my mate. We are heavenly messengers and gifted with the power of speech. Let us fly back to our home in the skies.'

'Why should I let such a rare and beautiful pair of golden swans go? You will be the showpiece of our kingdom and the envy of every other King,' said Nal.

'If you release us, in return we will lift the burden that for many days now has been weighing your heart down,' said her mate.

'What burden are you talking about, my golden beauty?' asked Rudra. 'What is weighing heavily on my dear friend's heart?'

'Only a woman can divine what is in a man's heart,' said the pen.

'And only a man can gaze deep into a woman's to see what is her heart's desire,' answered her mate.

'If you spare my mate's life and let us go, Prince... I will fly above the Vindhyas to Kundina, the opulent capital of Vidarbha. That is where your heart longs to fly, isn't that so? I will find my way to Damayanti's chambers and apprise her of your godlike form and handsome good looks, of your many qualities... of how your eyes keep searching for her everywhere... how your heart beats only for her. I will fill her heart with love and longing for you, O Prince!'

'Will you really be able to accomplish that?' asked Nal.

'Trust me... I am gifted with the power of eloquent and persuasive speech,' answered the swan confidently.

'So fly away now, my handsome golden-winged swan,' Nal said. On the spur of the moment, he unclasped the precious pearl necklace he was wearing and looped it around the swan's neck. 'Give this as my gift to the beautiful lady. Meanwhile your mate will stay with me until you return with glad tidings. Fear not for her, she will be our royal guest and be well looked after. Upon your return, both of you will be free to go wherever you wish.'

The male swan lovingly pecked his mate and spreading his golden wings flew southwards. They all stood watching until it was just a golden speck in the sky and then finally disappeared over the Vindhya mountains, on its way to the kingdom of Vidarbha.

A deep sigh escaped from the swan who had stayed back and she looked crestfallen. Seeing her look so forlorn, Nal's heart melted, 'Come, come… don't be sad. He will soon be back after fulfilling his mission. Come, meet the Queen Mother, she will be thrilled to meet you and shall feed you the most precious pearls.'

Rudra added his two bits to that. 'We have heard that swans love to feed on pearls.'

The swan bowed her neck. 'That is most gracious of you Prince,' she said with a hint of a smile. 'But if we were to swallow pearls… surely they would get stuck somewhere in our long necks…we would choke on them and die!'

Rudra roared with laughter at the swan's response. Nal smiled at the bird, 'You combine both beauty and wit, my lovely bird of paradise!'

'However, I am willing to give crushed and powdered pearls in a goblet of wine a try,' replied the swan. 'For I, on the other hand, have heard that young maidens of your tribe drink that to preserve their youth and glowing beauty… well into old age.'

'Come, let us get confirmation on that from my beautiful mother,' laughed Nal. 'And, if she says she also partakes of that concoction occasionally, then you can drink as many goblets as you wish.'

Chapter 5

THE GO-BETWEEN

Soaring smoothly over the peaks of the Nishadha range including the Nila and Shweta mountains, the snow-white swan paused only once to drink the energising waters of the Payoshini River before he took flight again. He now flew southwards over the Vindhya mountains, letting out an excited 'hoo-hoo' upon sighting the kingdom of Vidarbha. He slowed down, moving into a gliding motion and circled over the golden domes of the palace at Kundina to find an appropriate place where he could land unseen by the palace guards. *Perhaps it would be best to wait for a while hidden in the foliage of the jambul (jamun) tree,* he thought. He bent his wings to slow his approach, landing smoothly on its branch, unseen by anyone. Hungry after the long flight, he picked at bunches of the purple fruit of the tree being careful to spit out the seeds where they would not attract too much attention. He waited patiently for the high noon sun to lower itself in the sky and with half-closed eyelids dozed on his secure perch.

The loud, brassy clang of a gong being struck snapped him out of his afternoon nap and he cocked his head to ascertain the direction of the sound that echoed through the palace and even sent a slight shudder up his tree. He saw a group of giggling maidens come prancing out into the gardens.

'Goodness!' he heard two of them exclaim. 'It's still quite warm out here! Come, let's dip our feet into the fountain there.'

'Ha! Warm indeed!' the swan muttered to himself. 'They should see how hot it is from where I have just come!'

'Where are Damayanti and Chitra, do you know?' someone asked.

'I heard Damayanti had another sitting for a portrait being done of hers,' Ritika volunteered.

'Damayanti will be joining us soon,' said Chitra coming up to them while fanning herself with a hand-held fan of peacock feathers. 'She is changing out of the heavily-embroidered clothes and jewellery she was wearing for the portrait. The painter has just left. Come, let us go and sit in the shade of that pagoda near the flowing stream... it will be cooler there.'

Overhearing this, the swan mentally blessed Chitra for providing him with an opportunity to go into the palace unseen. He flew down from his perch and in the direction from which the girl had come a while ago. Seeing a palace maid coming out of a chamber carrying some clothes, he hid behind a huge flower pot to escape being noticed. As soon as she was out of sight, he flapped his wings and flew to the window and perched on its ledge and let out a soft 'hoot'.

On hearing the sound, Damayanti, who was clasping a bracelet around her delicate wrist almost dropped it to the floor. She whirled around to see the swan giving several bows with its long, graceful neck. She stood rooted to the spot, not believing her ears as she heard the swan ask in husky tones, 'Do I have permission to enter your chambers, Princess?'

'I've heard of talking parrots, but a swan that can speak... and that too in my language! You must be extraordinarily gifted, you lovely bird!' said a surprised Damayanti. 'Of course, you may enter!'

'You are most gracious, Princess,' the swan said, thanking her. 'But what I have to convey to you cannot go beyond these curtained walls. May I request you to close the door?'

'From where have you come, my golden-winged bird? The swans in our kingdom are all white-feathered and I have never heard of, or seen a swan with golden-wings,' enquired Damayanti.

'We are a special breed of heavenly messengers and are gifted with the power of speech. A bevy of us were migrating during the harsh winters of Mansarovar to warmer climes. We paused to rest our tired wings in the refreshing waters of the Payoshini River at Giriprastha, the capital city of Nishadha. There in the palace gardens, my mate and I were captured by Prince Nal, who…'

'Prince Nal of Nishadha?' exclaimed the Princess. 'I have heard his name and am told that he is a prince among men…'

'Prince...? Prince...? My dear lady, he is like unto a god! A godlike countenance… a godlike bearing…' gushed the swan. 'But, my fair lady, praises of your beauty are sung not only on earth but also among the gods in heaven!'

'Ah-hh… you are too kind but there is no need to flatter me, gracious swan,' demurred Damayanti while patting his head. 'I had heard that swans in heaven are fed on pearls, but I didn't know they also adorned their necks with these lovely beads,' she added while running her fingers over the pearl necklace.

The swan appeared to smile and let out a hoot of laughter. 'I am just the courier of this lovely necklace. I bear a message from Prince Nal and this pearl necklace is a gift from him to you. Although, I must say that the lustre and sheen of your radiant skin far outshines that of these precious and rare pink pearls. Please do me the favour of removing this necklace from my neck and drape it around your lovely neck, Princess.'

'But I cannot accept such a priceless gift… and that too from someone I don't know and have never met,' protested Damayanti.

'Yet, he is the man who comes to you in your dreams, just as you are the woman who haunts him day and night,' the swan replied. 'How do I know this you may well ask, Princess? I know this because of my divine powers of perception…

I can look deep into the minds and hearts of people and can wager my golden feathers, that you two are made for each other. Yours is a match truly made in heaven!'

'I really don't know…' murmured Damayanti.

Seeing her hesitate, the swan decided to capitalise on her wavering mind and, adopting another ploy, said in a plaintive voice, 'Besides, the Prince of Nishadha has, not to put a harsh word on it, my mate as a hostage. If I do not return with my mission accomplished, I will surely bear the brunt of his disappointment and he may decide not to give us our freedom.'

'Oh dear!' exclaimed Damayanti. 'He cannot do that! From whatever you have told me about him, he appears to be of a kind and noble character.'

'Yes, he is all that and more…' the swan nodded his head. 'But one can never tell what a man may do when his gift of love has been spurned…'

'Well, I certainly don't want to put your freedom in peril,' declared Damayanti. She bent forward to unclasp and unwind the pearl necklace adorning the swan's neck. 'It is lovely indeed… the pearls have a unique inner glow to them,' she remarked running the strand of pearls through her fingers.

'If your beauty, which is unrivalled, needed any adornment, then I swear to everything I hold dear that this is the perfect complement to it,' the swan smiled. 'And, crowning it all is your tender and compassionate heart.'

'Oh, you flatter me too much!' laughed Damayanti. 'Wait here for me, I shall be back soon.'

Damayanti called for a maid to bring a bowl of fresh water and a few plump, juicy jambuls. 'You must be hungry and thirsty after your flight. Have some of the fruit and slake your thirst.' She then stepped nimbly towards an inner chamber and returned with a small scroll that she tied to the swan's right foot with a tasseled thread of gold.

'Be sure to deliver this personally to Prince Nal as a token of my regard, and as an appreciation of his lovely gift. He will understand the message the scroll holds for him,' she said with a coy smile.

'Rest assured, your message will delivered safely, Princess,' the swan replied. Then he bent his head and with his beak plucked out a golden feather from his wing. 'Will you kindly accept this golden feather as my gift to you? I would feel honoured if you do.'

'Oh, that's a lovely gesture! I thank you, kind sir,' exclaimed a delighted Damayanti.

'May I now have your permission to return to Nishadha?' asked the swan with a gracious bow.

'Can't you stay the night and tell me more about Prince Nal?'

'Much as I would have loved to, I know the Prince will be anxiously awaiting my return to know the outcome of his mission,' answered the swan.

'That's fine then... take good care on your flight to Nishadha. Oh! And please see the scroll doesn't come untied along the way!'

'Don't worry, Princess... your message will be safely delivered to the Prince,' assured the swan. He hopped onto the window ledge and spreading his wings, took flight.

Chapter 6

Pangs Of Love

The sun was low on the horizon and the chirp and twitter of birds was now muted as they were flew home to their nesting places among the jasmine and jambul trees. King Virasena was enjoying a quiet evening stroll with his Queen in the palace gardens.

'After the hustle and bustle of everyday living... as the sun sets slowly behind the hills... everything seems to start winding down. The flowers begin to close their petals... the fish in the ponds swim more lazily. It's almost as if the day is folding upon itself. A veil of peace seems to descend upon us at dusk,' mused the King.

'Hmmm... if only you could tear yourself away from affairs of State, we could be doing this more often,' rued Queen Vasumati.

'To tell you the truth, I am quite looking forward to the day when I can relinquish my kingship,' he sighed, letting out a deep breath.

'Well... Nal will be eighteen next year and ready enough to take on the mantle. You have seen to it that he has been well tutored in the arts of kingship, politics and affairs of State. We should really start thinking of his marriage. In fact, I have already put several matchmakers on the job of finding a suitable bride,' said the Queen Mother.

'Yes, once both our sons are married and have produced heirs... our familial responsibility will be more or less over. Then you and I can proceed onto the next phase of our lives together by taking up *vana-prastha*... our abode in some rishi's hermitage in the forest,' suggested Virasena.

'Then, at last, I shall have you all to myself,' she smiled.

'Twenty-four hours of the day... ? Won't you get fed up of me?' he laughed, then suddenly turning serious, he asked, 'By the way, I haven't seen much of Nal these past few days... where is he? Has he gone off on a long hunt somewhere with his friends?'

'No he hasn't... but I have noticed that he has been mostly keeping to himself these days... and looking a bit wan and lost as he strolls along the canal. Even his night lamp keeps burning, I am told, into the wee hours!' she said.

'Hmmm... what's up with the lad, I wonder? Is he in love? I think I shall have a word with Pushkar.'

'Oh! Pushkar won't know anything! If you really want to know what is going on in Nal's mind, probe his close friend Rudra... he keeps hinting of some maiden who is apparently haunting him in his dreams. Maybe you should have a word with him.'

A week had gone by since the golden-winged swan had brought the missive from Damayanti. With bated breath, he had unrolled it and had been quite stunned. The likeness was remarkable between the portrait Visheshwara had painted on the image drawn out of his dream, and the portrait which Damayanti had sent him. He was euphoric!

'So, what else did that golden swan have to tell you, Nal?' asked Rudra. 'Is she as beautiful as the rumours suggest?'

'All that... and then over and above whatever one has heard about her. He also said that they barely do justice to her beauty...

in fact, the swan himself was quite blinded by it! Here, you can judge for yourself,' offered Nal, unrolling the painted portrait Damayanti had sent through the winged messenger.

'Hmmm… not half-bad… she has a slight squint, methinks,' Rudra slyly commented, rubbing his chin, and letting out a loud guffaw.

'Squint!' Nal boxed his friend's ear. 'You are surely a cross-eyed rascal, yourself!' Then realising he was being teased, he lunged at Rudra and wrestled him to the ground. Panting and out of breath, Rudra freed himself at last and brushing his clothes, stood up.

'So, what happens next?' he asked.

'Only God knows what will happen next! Not much I expect!' Nal said in a dejected voice.

'How about I dressing as a peacock and entering her chambers with another gift of your love for her?' Rudra asked, his eyes dancing wickedly. He spread out his hands behind him mimicking the fan of the bird's tail and strutting around Nal.

'Oh please! Stop your clowning or I will really strangle you this time!' Nal remonstrated.

'And you stop behaving like a lovesick dope!' Rudra retorted. 'Hey, I have an idea! Why don't you abduct her and bring her here, just like the heroes of yore!'

'Shut up Rudra and keep your bright ideas to yourself,' Nal said with some exasperation. 'I'm lovesick, yes, but not yet mad enough to fall in with your harebrained ideas.'

'Okay, okay… relax… I will think of something,' cajoled his friend. 'Let me sleep over it.'

'I suggest you do that!' And, don't show me your ugly face till you have something worthwhile to offer,' sulked Nal.

'Hey, who are you calling ugly?' Rudra said in a hurtful tone. 'I am prettier than your lady-love.'

'So should I marry you instead?' Nal laughed and throwing his arm around Rudra's shoulders gave him a friendly hug and then a push to send him on his way.

Far away in Kundina, a lovelorn Damayanti was slowly becoming a shadow of her former bubbly self. It has been observed that when love becomes an all-consuming affair, it can be termed as a kind of sickness. She avoided the company of her sakhis and appeared lost in her own world. The blush had faded from her cheeks and her pallor was unhealthy. She looked melancholic as she wandered around in a daze in the palace gardens by herself, or languished in her chambers. Hushed whispers had begun to circulate that something was amiss with the lovely princess. Her companions had tried everything they could think of that would break through this shell she seemed to have withdrawn into. They had actors stage humorous skits, invited renowned classical singers to lift her spirits with melodious ragas, the royal cooks use their culinary arts to prepare tempting dishes to tickle her palate, but nothing seemed to work.

Murmurs of his sister's strange affliction reached the ears of her brother Dana. Chitra, who was engaged in a romantic dalliance with him had, in a weak moment, confided that perhaps Damayanti's aloofness had something to do with the appearance of the golden-winged swan she had mentioned to her some weeks ago. 'If you ask me,' she added, 'I think she is nurturing a love in her heart and pining away for someone we know nothing of. She is guarding it as a closely held secret to her bosom.'

'What nonsense, Chitra,' Dana scoffed. 'I agree she is looking somewhat lost these days, but that's only because she is missing our mother who, as you know, is away at her parents' place.'

'You men are so blind!' Chitra said, pinching his arm. 'Besides, you don't know what goes on inside a woman's heart.'

'Anyway, mother is arriving day after tomorrow,' said Dana. 'I will ask her to find out what Damayanti keeps daydreaming about. Being younger, I certainly cannot approach and ask her!'

'My goodness, Damayanti!' exclaimed her mother. 'How thin and pale you have become while I was away! Haven't you been eating properly, or have you been unwell?'

She turned to Damayanti's handmaidens. 'All of you have been very careless and not looked after her well. She is looking like a shadow of her former self!'

Damayanti let out a deep, long drawn-out sigh. 'Oh Mother, you really shouldn't be angry with them. They are not to blame...'

'Then who else can I blame? Tell me who else is responsible for this state of poor health that I find you in?' asked her mother with mounting concern.

'No one is to blame, Mother. You are worrying unnecessarily. Really, I am quite all right,' said Damayanti weakly. 'I just feel that I want to go away somewhere. I feel so confined, so restless. My heart longs for what... I don't know!'

'I am sending our royal physician to take a good look at you,' her mother said. Turning to her handmaidens, she ordered, 'You girls come with me. I am sending some fruit and energising potions for her and you have to see that she has them.'

Alone with her husband that night, Queen Charumati, having intuitively arrived at the cause of Damayanti's listlessness and long drawn-out sighing, remarked, 'Have you noticed how absent-minded our daughter has been looking of late?'

'Ha... what! What do you mean?' exclaimed King Bhima. 'I really haven't seen much of her since you have been away, my dear. You know, affairs of State...'

'Yes, yes... I know all that! It's your standard excuse when you want to avoid an issue,' smiled Charumati. 'But this is something that you cannot brush under the carpet.'

'So, what is it about Damayanti that's troubling you, my dear?'

'Like young maidens of her age, I think she is suffering

the pangs of love. Instinctively, I called her best friend Chitra to my chambers this evening to find out what was troubling Damayanti.'

'So? Did she have anything to reveal? I know you can worm out the best-kept secrets when you set your mind to it,' smiled King Bhima.

'Well, if it's something affecting my daughter, shouldn't I be concerned?' huffed Charumati. 'Anyway, Chitra blabbered something about Damayanti talking about a strange, golden-winged swan. Now, you tell me... have you ever heard of, or seen, a swan with golden wings!'

'Well,' laughed the King. 'Anything is possible... I always keep an open mind!'

'Stop being facetious, husband!' chided Charumati. 'She also mentioned that the swan gave her a pearl necklace. And... I saw a pearl necklace, which neither I, nor her brothers, have gifted her, hanging around her neck!' she said with a note of pride in her detection skills.

'So why didn't you simply ask her where she got it from, my dear?' suggested the King.

'Hush... when broaching delicate matters of the heart, one cannot be so blatant. They have to be handled with velvet gloves, tact and a measure of discretion,' answered the Queen. 'So what I have to suggest is this...'

'And your 'this' is 'that'...?' laughed the King.

'Oh, stop treating it as a joke!' remonstrated Charumati. 'I think it is time we announced a swayamvara of Damayanti and sent out invitations to the princes and nobles of kingdoms far and near to attend. And...'

'And what?' he cocked an eyebrow.

'And treat this as an important matter of State,' she cajoled ruffling his hair.

King Bhima roared with laughter at her firm, but mildly issued, command.

Chapter 7

Mischief Of The Gods

After roaming the earth and having gathered all the information on how the kings were ruling over their lands and their subjects, it was time for the divine sages Narad and Parvata to ascend to the temperate climes of heaven and also escape the scorching summer winds that were blowing across Vidarbha. As they approached *swarga*, Lord Indra's heaven, the white, fleecy clouds dispersed to reveal the golden gates that were opening slowly in welcome. The two sages floated down and entered the court of Indra.

Strumming his single-stringed *tanpura*, Narad, in his customary way of announcing his arrival by the constant repetition of Lord Vishnu's other popular name, chanted, 'Naa-raayan… Naa-raayan! We are so happy to see all the gods gathered here today, aren't we, Parvata? How come there is not the usual bickering going on? Is there peace in heaven, as there is on the earth we have just left behind us?' asked Narad with an amused expression, strumming his tanpura again for added emphasis.

The Lord of swarga slapped his thigh and laughed, 'Your arrival is always looked forward to Narad Muni and, for once, you can spare us your barbed witticisms.' The *apsaras,* the beautiful nymph-like court dancers of swarga, tittered.

'It's good to know that the kings of earth are not bickering, as is their wont, Narad Muni. So, pray tell us, what is the reason for this bonhomie and goodwill prevailing among the kings this time? Is it because some big festival is approaching?' Indra remarked with a tinge of sarcasm.

Narad smiled and turning to look at the gathered assembly, plucked a few quick notes on his tanpura. Then he addressed them, 'An event, far more exciting than any festival, has been announced by King Bhima of Vidarbha.'

At this, Lord Vayu piped up enthusiastically, 'Is he organising one of his famous chariot races and all the kings and princes are thrilled to be participating in it? I hear it is something worth seeing!'

'A pretty good guess, my Lord, but it's not the race that is exciting them, nor it is the accompanying prize and the honour of winning it. This time, it is the event that will mark the culmination of the chariot races,' Narad said cryptically.

'Come, come… now stop teasing our curiosity. What is it that could entice the king and princes to participate in the race, instead of their champion charioteers?' asked Lord Agni.

'It is the trophy, my Lords. It is the hand of the beauteous Princess Damayanti in marriage. Her swayamvara is the crowning event of the festivities. Even as I speak, Kundina, the capital city, is being decked with pennants and the flags bearing the royal insignia of the invitees. The ambassadors of King Bhima are riding out to various kingdoms far and near carrying the invitations for the swayamvara, bearing the portrait of princess Damayanti,' elaborated Narad.

Parvata coughed politely into his fist and cleared his throat as if to speak. 'Er-rr… if I may be allowed to speak, my Lords…'

'Of course, Rishi Parvata,' said Lord Indra with a graceful gesture of his hand, and a nod towards Narad Muni.

Narad gave his trademark mischievous smile. 'Parvata always has some interesting tidbits to add! What will it be this time, my friend?' He wondered if he had somehow missed out on some interesting gossip during his sojourn on earth.

'My Lords, during my stay at the palace of King Bhima, I was taking an evening stroll in his gardens when I overheard some maidens talking among themselves. From what I gathered, it seems that the Princess Damayanti has already lost her heart to the prince of Nishadha.'

'Who? You mean Nal of Nishadha; that small kingdom, if it can be called that, just north of the Vindhyas? What chance does he stand when pitted against the magnificent kingdoms of Kosala and Magadha to name just two!' scoffed Indra.

'Yes, my Lord. Prince Nal is reputed to be the most handsome man among mortals,' averred Parvata. 'Just as Damayanti is rumoured to be the most beautiful maiden on earth.'

'You mean you did not get an opportunity to see Princess Damayanti during your stay at the palace? Surely you did, Parvata,' joked Narad.

Parvata blushed furiously and broke into a sweat. Grinning sheepishly, he said, 'Of course I did, Narad Muni.'

'Even more beautiful than my apsaras here?' exclaimed Indra.

'Let me say that she would be a lovely adornment to your swarga,' Narad remarked tactfully.

Turning to the assembled gods, Indra asked, 'Then why don't we make a bid for Damayanti's hand and attend her swayamvara? Being gods, we are above mere mortals, so we can just land up there without a special invite. King Bhima is bound to receive us with pride and honour at his daughter's swayamvara, and may the best among us gods win her hand.'

'Hear, hear!' a cheer resounded from the assembled gods. 'Can a mere mortal even hope to compete with our eternal youth and beauty? Never… ever!'

Narad Muni turned to Parvata and whispered, 'Just wait till they see Nal… they are all so high on soma and lost in their own delusions!'

'Shssshhh… someone will hear us and take offence. We don't want to lose our own divine status! I, for one, don't want to be expelled from Indra's swarga!' said an alarmed Parvata.

A hush had suddenly fallen in Indra's court. Fearing that Narad's outpouring into his ear had been overheard, Parvata began rambling, 'Look-look! Agni, Varuna and even Yama are coming towards us!'

'Indra has also stepped down from his throne, Parvata!' nudged Narad.

'We are really done in by our indiscretions this time,' quavered Parvata.

'Smile... Smile... put on a good face,' Narad hissed at him.

Then turning to face the luminous four approaching him, he strummed his tanpura and beamed at them, 'Naa-raayan... Naa-raayan!'

Coming up to Narad, the gods joined their hands in pranam. Indra, being the spokesman, said, 'Divine Messenger of us gods, Narad Muni, we seek your advice. Do you think one of us can win the hand of Damayanti, she whom you say is a rare pearl among women?'

'You are the King of swarga, my Lord, and these are your companion gods. I see no reason why you cannot bid for her hand,' replied Narad, cleverly evading a direct answer. 'However, in this case, a clear answer will only come from the princess herself. Who she will honour with her *varmala*, the matrimonial garland of flowers, only she will decide.'

'She will choose one of us, of that we are certain,' Agni made bold to answer. 'After all, she will enter swarga through marriage with one of us.'

Parvata cleared his throat. 'Ahem-mm... it stands to reason that the most beautiful woman would want to marry the most handsome man. If we are to believe the rumours, they suggest that the most handsome man appears to be a mortal by the name of Nal.'

A stunned silence greeted his remark. Narad shifted uncomfortably at Parvata's indiscretion. *That young man has yet to learn the art of tactful evasion, he is just too outspoken,* he thought, and made a mental note to advise him to hold his tongue.

Varuna arched an eyebrow at Parvata. 'Can a mere mortal compete with the beauty and eternal youth of a god?'

'My Lord, he is not the one competing… it appears to me that it is you gods who are competing,' Parvata blustered on, regardless.

Vayu blew a whiff of air to cool down what appeared to be an argument that was unnecessarily getting heated. 'Let's all calm down a bit. And Parvata is not wrong either when he say it is we who are competing. Of course we are competing for the hand of the fair Damayanti.'

At this boost of support, Parvata squared his shoulders and looked Varuna in the eye, a trace of defiance reflecting in his gaze. Narad Muni rolled his eyes heavenward. Then realising that he was already in heaven, he sniggered at his own silliness. However, he decided to now intervene. 'As they say, all is fair in love… and war,' mused Narad. 'And this swayamvara is going to be a blend of love, strategy, and skilful tactics. He who is mindful of all these and uses them to his advantage will undoubtedly carry the day… and carry away Damayanti as his bride.'

'Hear, hear!' the four gods cheered in unison.

'Well, both Parvata and I are thankful for the welcome extended to us, Lord Indra,' said a gracious Narad. 'However, we are quite exhausted from our travels and would like your permission to retire to our chambers, if you will allow us.'

Indra turned towards a bevy of apsaras in the galleries above and called out, 'Rambha… Sonakshi… come forward and kindly escort these venerable sages to their chambers and see to their refreshments.' Then turning to Narad, he said, 'You have earned a well-deserved rest Narad Muni, as has Parvata here. Go now and rest. My lovely apsaras here will see to your every comfort.'

Then turning towards his companions, he said genially, 'Come with me Agni, Varuna and Vayu… let us devise a foolproof strategy to upset Nal's apple cart, and ensure that only one of us wins the hand of the lovely Damayanti.'

Chapter 8

The Princess Takes A Bold Step

The excitement was palpable. Kundina throbbed and pulsated with the frenzied preparations underway for the upcoming swayamvara of its lovely Princess. But the one who should have been at the centre of it all was distraught and in the throes of despair.

'This just won't do Damayanti,' exclaimed a concerned Chitra. 'How long are you going to keep moping and sighing... what good is that doing? Your swayamvara is just a few moons away and here you are sitting idly with your hands folded in your lap!'

'But what else can I do?' Damayanti wailed. 'How can I get a message across to Prince Nal to make sure he attends the event? That golden swan is probably somewhere far away at Mansarovar lake and oblivious of my plight.'

'It's now or never... we must quickly get the word across to him!' said an agitated Chitra. 'Let us think, think, think. But, wait a minute... isn't that maid of yours... what's-her-name... Bharati... from Nishadha? Yes! Therein lies our answer.'

'What does she have to do with this?' queried Damayanti.

'Let us send her to Nishadha. She will be your messenger to Prince Nal. Get that golden feather the swan gave you Damayanti. That will be a clear message from you asking him to hurry towards Kundina. By now, the news of your approaching swayamvara must have reached his ears, too!'

Excited at the ploy, Damayanti brought out the golden feather and a scroll bearing her portrait. Placing the feather in it's centre, she rolled up the scroll and told Chitra to get her a stick of wax and her ring with which to seal the package. She then sent for Bharati, who came running as soon as she got the summons.

'You sent for me, Princess?'

'Yes, Bharati. I wish to send you on a personal mission to Nishadha. You are to deliver this scroll in the hands of Prince Nal and, mind you, no one else! You must find your way to the palace and the chambers of the prince, unseen by anyone. I have ordered the swiftest horse to be saddled for you, so you can make the journey fast. After delivering this scroll, you are to return as soon as you can. Here is a pouch with some gold coins that you may need on your journey. If you accomplish your mission speedily and successfully, there will be another pouch like this one waiting for you here,' Damayanti said while handing over the package to her.

'Don't worry, Princess. I'm a good horsewoman and will ride like the wind,' Bharati said with a self-assured air.

'Good girl!' commended Damayanti. 'Here, drape this cloak around you so no one recognises you when you leave and when you return to Kundina.'

'Hurry back as soon as you have delivered the message from the Princess,' added Chitra. 'And remember, not a word of this to anyone here!'

Nal was lying on the grass along the banks and lazily tossing pebbles into the canal that flowed through the gardens of the palace at Giriprastha, when a handmaiden of his mother came up and said that Her Highness wished to see him. Sighing, he got up and brushed the stray blades of grass from his clothes.

'Nal… there you are! Your father wants to meet both of us together in his chambers.'

'At this time of the day? What's it about mother?' Nal asked.

'Well, the only way to find out would be by going there, wouldn't it?' she smiled.

As they entered the King's presence, they saw a messenger of some neighbouring kingdom taking his leave and withdrawing from the audience chamber. Charumati glance briefly in his direction and raised an eyebrow at her husband.

'Did I see the royal emblem of Vidarbha on that man's ceremonial turban?'

The King smiled at her. 'Your eyesight is still very sharp and clear, my dear.'

'And what is that you are holding rolled up in your hand, my husband?' she queried.

'This,' announced King Virasena, 'is an invitation to us requesting the presence of our son, Prince Nal, at the swayamvara of King Bhima's daughter, Princess Damayanti.'

Nal's heart skipped several beats and then began thumping so rapidly and loudly in his ears that he was sure his father and mother could also hear its pounding. He took a couple of deep breaths to slow its pumping and hoped his parents hadn't noticed how the blush had spread across his neck and face till it seemed that it was almost on fire. Fortunately, his uncle entered at this point causing a diversion that for the moment took their attention away from him.

Nal's uncle, who had heard the king making the announcement as he was entering, beamed. 'Ah, that is a great honour indeed my brother. The kings and princes of much larger and more reputed kingdoms than ours will be part of this august gathering, bidding for the hand of Princess Damayanti in marriage. Yes, yes, it is indeed a great honour King Bhima is bestowing on us by inviting Prince Nal for the swayamvara.'

King Bhima turned to Charumati and smiled. 'What do you have to say to this, my Queen? It's for some time now that you have been talking about the matter of Nal's marriage. So it seems, the gods have heard your prayers and are going to fulfill your wish. That is, if Nal proves himself worthier than all the others and wins the hand of the princess in marriage.'

Charumati's chest swelled with pride as she put a motherly arm around her son's shoulders and declared, 'There is none worthier than my son, dear husband… none worthier!'

The smile hadn't left Nal's face as he walked with his head in the clouds from his parents' chambers. Turning a corner, he bumped into Rudra.

'I have been looking all over for you, Nal! I have just heard…'

'What have you just heard?' asked Nal, his eyes dancing joyously.

'Oh, come on, you know how I love to lurk around doorways and eavesdrop on whatever talk goes on behind them. How else do you think I am able to entertain you with all the gossip doing the rounds of our palace?' Rudra asked, grinning from ear to ear.

'So what's the latest gossip your donkey ears picked up?' laughed Nal.

'I heard that a royal stallion is being trained to be sent as a gift to the kingdom of Vidarbha,' Rudra said cheekily.

'And, pray, what are you looking so thrilled about?' asked Rudra. 'Your eyes are sparkling so… so merrily!'

'Am I not always happy to see you, Rudra? You are the light of my eyes,' Nal retorted.

Both the friends slung arms around each other's shoulders and sauntered away towards the gardens.

That evening, as the sun went down and the attendants were going on their rounds to light the torches in the passages and hallways of the palace and the handmaidens were lighting lamps in the royal chambers, a cloaked figure entered from a secret passageway and tiptoed silently towards Prince Nal's private chambers. It huddled in a corner, ears straining to hear if any footfalls were approaching. Then darting a quick glance to its left and right to make sure no one would suddenly appear around the corner, it swiftly moved into the outer hall that led to the inner bedchamber of the prince. Hearing the animated conversation of two men approaching, the figure hid behind a draped tapestry.

'Well, I will bid you good night here, Nal... it is getting to be quite dark and I should be getting home.'

'Good night Rudra, and thank you for being such a good friend... see you tomorrow, early morning. We have to exercise the horses.'

Nal entered and began unclasping the heavy copper-and-leather belt around his waist. Removing the strands of pearls around his neck, he bent to place them on a side table. His eyes widened in surprise as he noticed a golden feather lying there. *Where did that come from?* he wondered, rubbing his chin. He picked it up and twirled it in his hand.

'It has come all the way from Kundina, Prince Nal,' he heard a feminine voice say, as the cloaked figure stepped out from behind the tapestry.

Startled, Nal swung around in the direction the voice had come from. In the low lamplight, she came forward and removed the hood of the cloak that was covering her face.

'I did not want to leave this on the table in case it fell into the wrong hands,' she said. 'And I have a personal message from the princess of Kundina to deliver to you.'

'How did you gain entry into the palace grounds?' Nal asked.

'The palace guards know me as I used to work here some years ago. I was a just a young girl at that time and used to accompany my mother who was a handmaiden to your mother, Queen Vasumati.'

Nal picked up a small wick lamp that was burning in an alcove and brought it closer to her face.

'I remember you… aren't you… Bharati? What are you doing in Kundina? asked Nal, taking the scroll from her hands.

'Yes, your Highness… I am Bharati… it's very kind of you to remember. I went to Kundina after my marriage to a man who was employed as a personal bodyguard of King Bhima.'

'How is the Princess Damayanti? What message do you carry from her?'

'The Princess has requested that you come as quickly as possible to Kundina. The preparations for her swayamvara are in full swing and she wants you to come and claim her hand in marriage,' said Bharati.

'Go and tell the Princess that we have received the official invitation for her swayamvara and I shall be leaving shortly for Kundina,' instructed Nal. 'But you have come a long way and need to rest before you make the journey back.'

'I am staying with my mother, Prince Nal. I shall leave for Kundina in the morning.'

Nal moved to a wooden chest that stood in a corner. He opened a drawer and took out a pouch of silver coins. Giving this to Bharati, he said, 'Take this, it will speed your journey back to the Princess.' Then something occurred to him and he removed a ring from his finger. 'Give this to the Princess; tell her it is my pledge that I will come to win her hand at Kundina.'

Bowing graciously, Bharati took her leave and melted into the shadows in the corridors as she made her way home.

Chapter 9

Waylaid By The Gods

From the east came Indra, carrying *vajra* – his thunderbolt in hand. The chief of the *devas* or gods, Indra rode atop his majestic mount Airavat – the four-tusked, white elephant. From the west came Varuna, Lord of the waters and the celestial ocean, riding *makara* – the jaw-snapping crocodile. From the south-east came Agni, Lord of fire, riding a *mesa* – the head-butting ram with its curved horns. And, last but not the least, came Yama from the south, swinging a noose in his hand, atop his mighty, black-skinned, water buffalo.

'Sorry, I'm a bit late,' apologised Yama. 'This buffalo of mine has grown just too fat and plods along really slowly.'

'Come on, let's hurry up now... as it is we have wasted enough time hanging around in the clouds of Mount Meru,' pleaded an agitated Agni.

'Look who is burning up in desire for Damayanti!' laughed Varuna. 'He looks as if he will burst into flames any second!'

'Enough of this tomfoolery, fellow devas,' Indra said briskly. 'Let's hasten to earth and halt Prince Nal's advance on Kundina.'

'But how will we recognise him?' queried Yama.

'Didn't Narad say something to the effect that he was more handsome than all of us put together?' Agni said billowing twin trails of blue smoke from his flared nostrils.

'No, it was Parvata who implied it! The cheek of that fellow, to equate an earthling with us gods!' huffed Varuna.

'Stop, stop!' commanded Indra. 'Let's not bicker about something we know nothing about. Let's first catch up with him… he must already be somewhere half-way up the road to Kundina!'

As the four of them hovered above a crossroad, an exasperated Agni asked, 'Now which of these four roads lead to Kundina?'

'Let me ask that farmer plowing his field. You all must hover around unseen. We don't want to frighten the poor country bumpkin with elephants and crocodiles appearing out of nowhere. He won't suspect me coming along riding on a buffalo,' advised Yama.

Quickly shape-shifting into a humble peasant, Yama approached the farmer and greeted him in the local dialect. 'Bhau, can you tell me which of these four roads lead to Kundina?'

'Why?' asked the yokel, in the inquisitive manner of all earthlings. 'What business do you have there?' Eyeing Yama up and down, he guffawed, 'Don't tell me you are also going for the Princess's swayamvara!'

It was all Yama could do to control his rage and not deal a death blow to the lout. He managed a laugh, 'No, no… I have a wife back home… I am going to Kundina on some work.'

The farmer winked and patted Yama's buffalo. 'Just pulling your leg, bhau… it's just that since the last few days a lot of people have been asking for the road that leads to Kundina as the crossroad here tends to confuse them. Well… you just take that road over there,' he said pointing in the southerly direction.

'Oh, and by the way, has anyone else been asking for directions today although it's a bit early in the morning to be riding out,' Yama asked in an off-handed voice.

'Now that you mention it, a handsome young man rode up in a chariot a while ago. I thought some god had descended from above!' said the peasant pointing his finger at the sky.

'Only a god could look so very handsome or *atishsya dekhana* as we would say around here.'

'Well, he must be a princeling or something,' Yama said casually. 'Now, *he* must surely be headed for the swayamvara!'

'I agree, bhau… I swear that any woman, married or unmarried, who set her eyes on him would lust for him,' the farmer added suggestively.

Yama shuddered inwardly at this rustic bawdiness. *How uncouth can these earthlings be!* he thought to himself, quite forgetting the fact that the motive for the four of them wasn't quite pure either. Thanking the farmer, he struck the flank of his buffalo with the noose and headed down the southerly road. Once he was safely out of the farmer's sight, he signalled the three gods hovering invisibly above that it was safe to land. Once their feet touched the ground, they dispensed with their mounts, while Indra conjured up chariots and horses for each of them.

'Well, I have something to tell you all,' said Agni. 'That peasant Yama sought directions from, wasn't wrong. I have seen Nal, and he is everything that Narad, Parvata and even that peasant had to say. Nal is indeed extraordinarily handsome.'

'And, how can you possibly know that, Agni?' asked Yama.

'You forget Yama, that whenever a yajna is held by earth people, a sacrificial fire is lit into which they proffer offerings of clarified butter, spices and condiments, grains and fruits, to me. My presence is invoked for the successful completion of the yajna. Therefore, whenever King Virasena and Queen Vasumati have performed the fire sacrifice, I have been present and have seen Nal grow as a young boy whenever he participated in the yajna. I have to admit he is even beyond mere handsome. Besides, it is not just a matter of looks. He is righteous, upright and a man of many talents. If it wasn't for us also competing for the hand of Damayanti, he would have no contest and would win hands down.'

'Well, let us catch up with him then and tell him to withdraw from the contest,' said Indra haughtily.

Nal reined in the horses to slow them down and swerved his chariot off the dusty mud road. The noonday sun blazed hot and bright overhead and he decided to rest awhile in the welcoming, cool shade of a peepal tree. He led the horses to water at a nearby stream and then tethered them in the shade of a tree nearby. Stripping off sweat-soaked garments, he waded into the stream.

Meanwhile, the gods were closing the distance between them and Nal. Suddenly, Agni who was in the lead raised his hand indicating to the gods behind him to slow down. 'Look!' he called out to the others, 'these tracks of a chariot signify that the rider has driven off onto a side road.'

Varuna came up to look and then sniffed the air. 'I smell a water-body somewhere nearby. He must have paused to water his horses, I think…'

'Come on then, let us scout around,' said Yama.

Indra was the first to spy the horses tethered to the tree. 'Shhh…' he whispered, indicating to the others not to make a noise. 'Let us close in on him and first see for ourselves if he is all that he is made out to be.'

Upon hearing the whinnying of his horses, Nal rose from the waters, pushing back the wet hair from his brow. Clad only in a loincloth that clung wetly to his thighs, he stepped ashore, droplets of water reflecting golden on his fair skin in the radiant, afternoon sun.

The gods grew wide-eyed and a collective gasp escaped their lips.

'Oh God! Such perfection in a mortal being!' exclaimed Agni.

'Why only Damayanti? Even my apsaras, Menka, Rambha, and Urvashi would give up swargalok for him!' said a peeved Indra.

'Stop gaping and being envious!' snarled Yama. 'Think of how we are going to get him to withdraw from the swayamvara.'

'Leave it to me,' said Indra stepping forward while the other followed behind.

Seeing the four king-like personages approaching, Nal greeted them with folded hands. 'Welcome friends, have you also come to water your horses and slake your thirst at the stream?'

'Yes, we halted here on our way to Kundina… you are Prince Nal of Nishadha, I think,' said Indra.

'Yes… I am also on my way to Kundina… but who may you all be?'

'We are the immortals, Prince Nal,' interjected Varuna. My companions are Agni, Yama and Indra – Lord of swargalok.'

Nal bowed low to pay his respects. 'I am truly blessed to be in your presence… but what have I done to deserve such an honour?'

'We have a mission that we want you to undertake on our behalf in Kundina,' answered Indra.

'Gladly… I will be happy to do whatever you ask,' Nal offered graciously.

'We are headed for the swayamvara of Princess Damayanti, and one of us hopes to win her hand in marriage,' continued Indra. 'Take our message to the Princess and convince her that she must choose one of us as her husband.'

The colour drained from Nal's face and then, just as suddenly, it flushed red. 'But I am myself attending the swayamvara to win her hand! How can I press your suit?' he sounded flustered. 'Princess Damayanti herself has sent a message asking me to be present at the occasion.'

'Will you dare to go against the wishes of the gods, Prince Nal? Besides, you have already given your word that you will gladly do whatever we ask,' Indra said. 'Does your word mean so little to you Prince Nal, that you will go back on it?'

Nal was cornered. There was no way he could go back on his word once he had voluntarily given it. 'So be it, my Lords. I shall do what you ask. But how will I be able to enter the Princess's private chambers before the day of her swayamvara?

It will be impossible for me to do that!'

'But it is possible for me to do just that,' replied Indra with visible glee at Nal's discomfiture. 'Nothing is impossible for gods!' he gloated.

Nal joined his hands and bowed to signify that he was submitting to the will and demand of the gods. 'I shall do as you wish and try my best to convince Princess Damayanti to choose one among you as her wedded husband.'

Indra raised his hand in blessing, closed his eyes and uttered a mantra. He then added, 'This mantra that I have just chanted will make you invisible, enabling you to enter the palace and the private chambers of the Princess unseen by the guards and the ladies in the women's quarters. Wait for the moment when she is alone and then as soon as you utter her name, you will become visible to her. The rest will be up to you and your skills of persuasion.'

Chapter 10

Nal Meets Damayanti

Nal entered the city gates of Kundina unseen as the sun was setting behind the Vindhya mountains. In the distance, he saw the burnished copper domes of the royal palace bathed in the reddish glow of sundown. In an annexe to the main palace building, he could make out the flags and pennants of the kingdoms of Kuru, Panchala and Kosala. This, he mused, meant that some of the kings and princes had already arrived and camped at Kundina in anticipation of Damayanti's swayamvara. The sound of temple bells and conch shells drew people towards the houses of worship for the evening rituals and aarti. Nal stayed close to the walls to avoid someone accidentally brushing against him and inched towards the palace.

It was just as well that he was invisible he thought, while negotiating the main buildings comprising the *sabhaghar* – the audience chamber of the king, and the offices of senior officials of King Bhima's court. Coming to an intricately latticed bamboo screen that ran the length of a long passage, he heard the faint laughter and chatter of women sporting in the grounds that lay beyond. Stopping now and again to peep through the openings in the bamboo screen, he observed maidens coming out of and entering various rooms and passageways. This gave him a fair idea of the layout of the women's quarters. Taking a deep breath, he stepped out into the open to move invisibly among the womenfolk.

'Arree Sugna, ruk... kahan bhaagi ja rahi hai?' he heard a pretty young girl asking another who was rushing past her, with some colourful stoles draped on her arm.

'Rajkumari Damayanti ne bulawa bheja hai, hat mere raaste se,' Sugna answered hurriedly and raced away.

Nal made a customary 'thank-you-God' auspicious sign by kissing the index finger of his right hand, touching it to his chest and raising it to his lips, and hurried off after Sugna. She dashed across a well-maintained garden that was abloom with flowers of every hue and dotted with fountains in which goldfish pouted and pink and white lotuses floated on large, green, circular leaves. Nal kept pace, following close on her hennaed heels. Sugna entered a pagoda-like structure known as *Saheliyon-ki-Badi* – a place where maidens usually met to dance, play or just while away the hours in small talk.

'Where will I find the Princess?' Sugna shouted across to a cluster of girls.

'In the back garden… both she and Chitra were on a swing,' said Maheswari.

'No-no,' said another. 'I've just come from there… they are not there any longer.'

'I saw her last in the *shringar kaksh* – her dressing room,' Nilambri shouted back, waving her hand.

'These girls!' huffed Nal, and followed Sugna as she headed towards the direction Nilambri indicated.

'Hato!' Sugna said pushing aside a guard posted at the door of the chamber. 'The Princess wants these urgently.'

'Give me a kiss and I will let you enter,' said the young guard grinning at her.

'Let me enter, and I will give you a kiss on the way out,' Sugna said saucily.

Nal couldn't help but smile at this delightful flirtation.

Then suddenly his brow furrowed and a confused look crept into his eyes. Something did not appear to be right. Why were all the girls dressed alike? He noted that their *ghagra-cholis* and dupattas were of the same cloth, colour and design. Why, even their hair was done in the same fashion and they wore identical jewellery! It appeared to be a deliberate charade of sorts. But to what end?

He followed the girl into the chamber. Here too, he noticed that everyone was similarly attired. It was difficult to make out who was Damayanti in their midst. Then his gaze fell on the reflection of the girl seated before a burnished copper mirror. A handmaiden was fixing a jewelled comb in her coiffure. He moved closer. He could now make out that the seated girl's features were similar to the portraits of the girl that hung on the walls. He stood riveted. Then the wheels whirred and clicked in his mind.

'Damayanti!' he gasped involuntarily.

As soon as the name escaped his lips, the cloak of invisibility fell from him.

Everyone's jaw dropped. They gaped, speechless.

Before any of the young girls could start screaming at the sight of a man in their midst, Damayanti recovered quickly and told Chitra to shut the front door immediately. She then instructed her to see that all the handmaidens left quietly through the back door, with a final word of warning that should anyone utter a word or dare to speak of this intrusion, they would have to pay for it with their life. She then turned to face Nal.

Before she could utter a word, Nal pre-empted her saying, 'Do not be alarmed, Princess… I would not dream of causing any harm… I have come here in this rather unusual manner at the behest of God Indra…'

'How could you mean me any harm, Prince Nal of Nishadha?' Damayanti answered without losing her poise.

Nal smiled. 'Yes, I am he… but how did you recognise me?'

'The golden-winged swan had described you to me in great detail… besides your renown precedes you, Prince,' Damayanti answered, her fingers playing with the pearl necklace around her neck.

This subtle action of drawing his attention to the necklace he had sent with the swan did not escape his notice and his eyes glowed with pleasure. 'And your painting really does not do you full justice, Princess,' Nal said with a winning smile, '...your grace and beauty cannot be captured by human hands.'

Determined to get a answer to the riddle that was nagging him, he said, 'But I am intrigued by something... why are all girls here, including you, dressed alike down to the very last detail? I was wondering how I would identify you among the others!'

Damayanti let out a peal of laughter. 'Well it's really quite simple, Prince. This charade or illusion was deliberately created so that I could move freely around the palace and the adjoining grounds to observe the various kings and princes who have come for my swayamvara. This way I could observe them at leisure without them becoming aware of my presence.'

'A very clever ruse, Princess,' Nal laughed. 'It even had me puzzled for a while...'

'Then how did you identify me?' asked Damayanti.

'Well, for one, that painted portrait you sent of yourself through the golden-winged swan. Then I saw the same likeness here adorning the walls of your chamber. And, finally, the portrait came to life as it were, when I saw your reflection in the mirror.'

'And, did you like what you saw... or rather, what you are now seeing?' she asked with a hint of a smile.

Nal looked adoringly at her, 'Do you even have to ask?'

Then suddenly remembering why he was actually there, he heaved a deep sigh and looked crestfallen.

Damayanti was quick to note the change in his expression. 'Why, what's the matter... what troubles you, Prince?'

'Alas... I don't know how to say it, Princess. My heart has been ripped out... torn apart...'

'What are you saying, Prince?' Damayanti was alarmed. 'Tell me clearly what is troubling you.'

'I still can't believe this has happened... I was on my way to attend your swayamvara when I got waylaid...'

Stepping forward, Damayanti asked, 'Waylaid by whom? The roads leading to the palace are well patrolled. There are no robbers or ruffians ...' Then seeing he was getting increasingly worked up, she said, '... you are looking quite pale... do sit here and calm down, while I get you a goblet of water.' She returned and handed it to him, saying, 'Here, drink this... now tell me who had the gall to waylay you!'

Nal held his head in his hands and looked morosely at Damayanti. He narrated how the four gods had accosted him on the road to Kundina and how each one of them had said that they were also coming to bid for the hand of the Princess. When they heard that Nal was also competing, they got very angry and told him in no uncertain terms to withdraw from the swayamvara. And then to top it all, how they had heaped the ultimate humiliation on him – through clever manipulation on Indra's part, they had compelled him to act as their messenger to inform the Princess that she must choose one among them as her husband during the swayamvara. Now, having given his consent to the gods that he would do their bidding – he was both duty-bound and honour-bound to keep his word. Done with unburdening himself, he looked helplessly at Damayanti, 'Tell me Princess how can I, who fell in love with you by simply hearing of the praises sung of your beauty, grace, virtue, and nobility of character, act otherwise knowing full well that my heart bleeds at the thought of losing you to one of those godly beings who have behaved in such an ungodly manner?'

'I too had heard the most wonderful things being said about you Prince Nal. And then one day, the golden-winged swan came bearing your message and this precious strand of pearls as a token of your love. From that very moment, I had, in my heart, accepted you as my husband. I will have no other. Therefore, I am also honour-bound and duty-bound to offer my marital garland to you as my husband of choice at the upcoming swayamvara, and that is a vow I hold most sacred. I will not let any god, let alone any mortal, make me sway from my dharma,' Damayanti said with determination.

'So, what is the solution to this predicament we both find ourselves in?' asked Nal. He spread his hands helplessly.

Taking his outstretched hands in hers, Damayanti assured him: 'Be of good cheer and courage, Prince. I see a way out, one in which the gods cannot lay any blame on you for not having fulfilled your given word to them. You will not bear the brunt of their displeasure,' assured Damayanti. 'Go back to them, and give them this message: 'Damayanti sends her regards and welcomes the gods to her swayamvara. She says that the person around whose neck she places the marital garland will be the husband of her choosing.'

She then went on to explain to Nal that on the day of the swayamvara, in the presence of everyone – kings, princes, rishis, nobles and, above all, the four gods waiting for that honour to fall on one of them, she would put the garland around Nal's neck. This way, there would no recriminations of any kind accruing to the Prince and he would, having fulfilled his word to the gods, come out blameless in the whole episode of the immortals pitted against mortals.

Nal sat upright and squared his shoulders. This time, he sighed with great relief. Damayanti with her single-minded focus had resolved the issue with tact, diplomacy and womanly insight. He felt that a heavy burden had been lifted from his heart. 'I should get going now… the gods will be waiting impatiently for my news.'

As he rose to leave, Damayanti stopped him. 'Wait, someone will see you if you walk out that door. That cloak of invisibility is not your shield anymore. Here, wrap this cloak around you… it will serve to protect your identity. There's a secret tunnel here which will take you out of the women's quarters and it opens discreetly into the busy city square.'

Nal smiled. 'Lead me to it, Princess.' At its entrance, he turned to hold her briefly in a quick embrace. 'I shall see you at the swayamvara.'

Chapter 11

STALEMATE

Strolling around like mortals in the busy streets and taking in the sights and sounds of Kundina, the gods were quite enjoying their sojourn on earth.

'It's rather nice, don't you think Varuna, to get away from the rarefied atmosphere of swargalok for a change?' remarked Agni.

'If you ask me, I was becoming rather restless always being surrounded by water. Not to mention the squabbles of the marine life which I am often called upon to resolve and that too to everyone's satisfaction!'

'Well, I have to personally make frequent trips to earth to escort some distinguished king or other mortal who has lived out his span of life here. So, it feels good to be here on a mission that promises to be far more entertaining and exciting,' smiled Yama.

'Where on earth is Prince Nal?' wondered Indra. 'What's taking him so long?'

'Who do you think Damayanti will choose from among us?' asked an impatient Agni.

Both Varuna and Yama kept quiet and exchanged sidelong glances. Yama, who was closest to him, nudged Agni with his elbow suggesting that he should douse his ardour in the presence of Indra, who after all was their Overlord. Varuna also expressed his disapproval with a frown at Agni's impetuousness. Abashed, Agni slipped behind the walkers.

Returning to their chambers, they were enjoying a tipple of *somarasa* – nectar of thc gods, when the guard announced a visitor.

'Welcome… welcome, Prince Nal!' greeted Indra. 'We have been anxiously awaiting your return… Were you able to meet Princess Damayanti and convey our wishes?'

'What did she have to say?' asked Agni, in his usual impetuous manner.

'What else could she have said?' Yama arrogantly turned to Agni. 'Which mortal wouldn't be thrilled to have an alliance with a god? Thrilled? She would in fact feel greatly honoured!'

'Come, come… let us first hear what Prince Nal has to tell us,' said Varuna.

Nal cleared his throat. 'Well… yes, I put your proposal to the Princess. She sends her greetings and has asked me to pay her respects and regard for each one of you. What's more, she is honoured that you will be competing for her hand at the swayamvara being held tomorrow. But…'

'But what?' asked Agni heatedly.

Nal nervously shifted his feet. 'She did not show any preference for any one of you, my Lords. She has asked that I personally escort you all into the wedding hall tomorrow, where she will garland the husband of her choice.'

Nothing escaped Indra's eye and he had noticed how nervously Nal shuffled his feet and avoided looking directly into their eyes while he was recounting his meeting with the Princess. *Something is amiss,* he thought. *Nal is hiding something*. But all he murmured, while tapping his chin, was a mild 'Hmm-mm…' Yet, hc could see that Nal was uncomfortable. He seemed to be inwardly grappling with something that was disturbing him. Indra gave him a nudge, 'Is that all Prince Nal… or is there anything else?' letting his words hang in the air.

His high sense of truth, moral worth and honour won over his initial reluctance of telling the gods what Damayanti had with chilling finality declared. Nal could not restrain himself and blurted it out. 'My Lord Indra... the Princess, in no uncertain terms affirms that since she loves only me and has mentally already accepted me as her would-be husband, she will not consider another – immortal or mortal. She will garland me in your gracious presence in front of the entire assembly.'

'What!' said an incredulous Agni. 'She will choose a mere mortal over an immortal god?'

'Has she taken leave of her senses?' asked a flabbergasted Yama. 'Or is she blinded by the beauty of this mortal being?'

Varuna remained unperturbed and shook his head in wonder. 'Who can fathom what goes on in a woman's mind? The more beautiful they are, the more defiant, proud and inscrutable they become.'

Indra, who had by now recovered from the way his plan had been foiled by the whim of a Princess, turned to Nal. 'Thank you, Prince Nal, for carrying our proposal to the princess. Of course, the final decision has to be that of Princess Damayanti and you are in no way to blame, or bear the responsibility, for its outcome. You have proved that you are indeed an honourable man.'

Nal, who had broken out in a sweat in the course of this exchange, mopped his brow and in his hurry to leave the presence of the gods dropped the painted square of cloth. Indra bent to pick it up, but noting out of the corner of his eye that it was embroidered with the royal crest of Kundina, he quietly slipped it under the folds of the silken stole draped over his shoulder.

Smiling at the departing figure, he turned to the other three gods and crooked a finger. 'Come,' he said. 'We have to plan and perfect our next move.'

'Next move?' queried Yama. 'Why is that necessary now?'

Indra arched an eyebrow and his gaze took in his three companions. 'Do you seriously believe that Damayanti is going to choose one of us? Don't be so deluded!'

'But… but! We are gods!' said an agitated Agni.

'So we are indeed, but let us not forget that Damayanti herself is born of a boon and that has probably gone to her head. She is a headstrong woman and a headstrong woman invariably follows the diktat of her heart,' offered Yama. 'And I should know… having dealt with Savitri – another such woman who outwitted even me!'

'That is why I am saying that we need to plan our next move very, very carefully. It has to be so brilliant that it cannot but succeed.'

Part 2

Webs of Conspiracy

Chapter 12

The Wily Gods

The 'World Protectors' as they were commonly known because they were the gods of the four directions – east, west, north and south – Indra, Agni, Varuna and Yama were now, late into the night, in the midst of formulating their strategy. Agni suggested they have their minions kidnap Prince Nal and hold him in a secret location until the swayamvara was over and done with and Damayanti had no other way out than to accept one of them. This was vetoed by the other three because as Yama pointed out, the Princess could well call off her swayamvara.

'No, no… I have a better idea,' Varuna said. 'Why don't we kidnap Damayanti instead and whisk her away to swargalok?'

'And thereby dig a watery grave for ourselves in your ocean?' scoffed Yama. 'The whole of *Vaikunth* (the heavenly abode of Lord Vishnu) will come down heavily upon all of us for outraging the modesty of a woman. Shiva will impale us on his trident!'

'Knowing his temper once he opens his Third Eye, that is quite likely to happen,' Indra commented wryly. 'Let's face it, we are after all junior or demigods and hence answerable to the Trinity for our actions.' Suddenly, Indra jumped up excitedly. He clapped his hands, 'That's it! That's it!'

'What's that? What's it?' the others chorused in unison.

'The face! *The face!*' Indra said. 'Don't you see? This whole thing hinges on *one* face!'

Varuna, Agni and Yama were flummoxed. They looked at each other and Agni shrugged his shoulders.

'Let me explain,' Indra said with barely concealed patience. 'If we rewind to the day when Narad and Parvata came visiting, what did they tell us? That Nal and Damayanti had been attracted towards one another merely… *merely*, mind you… about hearing praises of one another's looks and a few portraits painted by some artists! Nal and Damayanti hadn't really met until yesterday when we sent him as our go-between to Princess Damayanti.'

'And so? What does that lead to?' asked Agni, a bit riled.

'That leads to one inescapable fact,' replied Yama. 'Nal is more handsome than any, or all of us, put together.'

Indra clapped his hands in delight. 'Excellent! You hit the nail on the head, Yama.'

'Huh! What rubbish! More handsome than us?' grumbled Agni.

'He is… at least in Damayanti's eyes… and you know as well as I that beauty lies in the beholder's eye!' Indra said smugly.

'Even if we accept what you are saying, how does that in any way offer a solution?' queried Varuna.

'Close your eyes… all three of you, and start counting backwards from 10,' Indra said with a mischievous smile.

Privately, each one of them thought that this was no time for Indra to be playing games with them. But since he *was* their Overlord, they thought it best to humour him and complied with as much grace they could muster, with Varuna leading the countdown. When they heard him say '0' their eyes, like shutters, opened wide and their jaws dropped.

Standing in front of them was Prince Nal!

'What in heaven are you doing here, Prince Nal?' asked a shocked Yama.

'How on earth did you get here?' demanded Agni.

'Haha-haha-ha… you fools think you can win the hand of Damayanti in marriage?'

'Why, you... you rascal, how dare...' blubbered Agni and Yama.

'I dare because I am your Overlord!' Indra guffawed as he shifted back to his original self.

Their eyes blinked and popped as the three gods witnessed this act of deception.

'Don't you see?' asked Indra. 'What I can do... so can you! This is the only way we can hope to fool Damayanti into garlanding one of us at her swayamvara.'

Indra then elaborated on his plan. Reminding them that as gods they had the power to take on any form they desired under a given circumstance, he had thought up this foolproof plan to dash Prince Nal's and Damayanti's hopes of marrying one another. Confronted with five identical Nals, that is if the real Nal dared to defy them and also attend the ceremony, Damayanti in her confusion would be most likely to end up garlanding one among them. Varuna, Yama and Agni clapped each other on the back, marvelling at the brilliance of Indra's plan. With great gusto and glee, they accepted it enthusiastically. Before retiring to their respective chambers, Indra suggested that to complete the dissembling act, it was not enough to just look like a spitting image of Nal – they must practice to also walk and talk like the Prince.

The moon hung low in the sky as Nal, unable to sleep, paced restlessly in his chambers. He was on the horns of a dilemma. On one hand, although he had fulfilled the gods' directive to deliver their message to Damayanti, he was still reluctant to withdraw his suit. On the other hand, Damayanti had made it very clear that she had in her heart already accepted him as her would-be husband and declared she would place the ceremonial garland around his neck at the swayamvara that was to take place the next day.

What should he now do? Should he, to avoid any trouble, just leave Kundina and go home without contesting for her hand? What would his parents, the nobles of the court, and above all the populace of Nishadha, who were waiting for him to return with his bride, have to say? What face would he show them? They would all think he had turned tail and not risen to the challenge.

If he did not show up at the swayamvara tomorrow, not only would he lose face with all the kings and princes gathered there, he would have betrayed Damayanti's trust and, in her view, rejected her love. This, even after her assurance that she would find a way to resolve the issue without him incurring the wrath of the gods, when she would choose him over the four immortals. Above all, how could he, under the circumstances, stay true to his own dictum of always doing the 'right thing' according to his understanding of dharma?

What should I do? What should I do? he almost cried in anguish.

To quell his emotional turbulence, he reached out for the flask of sweet wine and filled the goblet lying next to it. He took a few sips to calm his nerves. He lay down on a couch and let its effects wash over him. The image of the golden-winged swan floated into his mind. If it wasn't for that swan, he mused, then this situation would not have arisen. Where was that bird, he wondered idly before his eyelids began to droop. The last image that arose in his mind was of the reassuring smile of Damayanti before he drifted off into a deep slumber.

It was one thing putting up a brave front in front of Nal. It was quite another, now that she was alone, to be confronted with what appeared to be a hopeless situation. Who would have thought the gods would also jump into the fray at her swayamvara? And that too, four of them! Were they crazy?

Did they want to trigger a revolt in Indralok if *one* among them, and naturally it would have to be only one of them, would somehow or the other win her hand in marriage? Damayanti shook her head.

'This is utter madness!' she said out aloud. She came out on the balcony and looked at the night sky. *Was their love already star-crossed?* the thought raced through her mind as she saw a shooting star streak across and then disappear somewhere in the distance. *Was that a good or a not-so-good omen?* she wondered. Another thought quickly followed on the tail of that one. *And, what in heaven's name were the gods thinking of... what on earth were they up to? Had they even thought their plan through? Did they want a civil war in Indralok – gods fighting with gods – just as kings fought with kings over territorial supremacy, or at times even over a beautiful woman? Or was it just a question of hurt pride and deflated egos that made them throw in the gauntlet into the swayamvara ring? Was it a direct challenge to men – in this case one particular man –that try all he may, he could not hope to win against a god?*

'Think... Think... Damayanti,' she muttered to herself as she hit her forehead repeatedly with her delicate fist. But nothing would come to her mind, which was already in such turmoil.

Chitra happened to be passing by and peeping in saw Damayanti was still up and awake.

'What's the matter? You should be sleeping... the swayamvara is tomorrow and you have to look fresh and glowing! Come on, lie down...'

'I'm feeling feverish, I think... can't sleep,' Damayanti said in a faint voice.

'Here, let me see...' said Chitra touching her forehead. 'It's just a case of nerves, don't you worry, all will go well. Now lie down, while I apply some cooling rosewater compresses to your forehead. Just relax.'

Damayanti sighed. 'Do me a favour Chitra... go to Prince Nal's chamber tomorrow early morning and make sure that he is present in the hall where the swayamvara is to be held.'

Chapter 13

Mirror Images

In the days leading to the swayamvara, the kings and princes had been entertained during the day by the champions of Kundina displaying their skills in archery, fencing, wrestling, martial arts, and chariot racing. Damayanti's three brothers, along with some of the younger princes of neighbouring kingdoms, had also joined in the fun and games and pitted their skills against the reigning champions. In the evenings, there had been lavish feasts and banquets hosted in turn by King Bhima, his sons, and his chief ministers, in honour of the visiting dignitaries and their guests. These had been accompanied by mind-boggling magic shows, music recitals, classical dance performances, and theatrical enactments of episodes from the rich treasury of ancient legends and folklore.

Today was the concluding day of the festivities. The air was heavy with the fragrance of incense mingled with that of spices and condiments required as offerings. As the sacred fire was lit with slivers of sandalwood in the copper havankund to the chants of the mantras led by the Brahmarishi Damana – Damayanti's three brothers, Dama, Danta and Damana (who was named after Brahmarishi Damana) kept dropping sacrificial offerings and pouring ladles of ghee to keep the fires crackling and burning bright. As the flames carried the aroma rising from the offerings to the gods in their respective heavens, they began to gather in the skies above Kundina. And from their respective guest chambers, the kings and princes of the land, who had come to attend the swayamvara, started entering the grand, gaily decorated hall. Each royal prince was announced and garlanded by a beautiful maiden and escorted to his respective seat.

While King Bhima and his Queen were seated on their royal thrones and observing the progress of the yajna, Damayanti was seated behind them separated by gauzy, translucent golden curtains embroidered with gold sequins. Rather than hiding her beauty, they only served to highlight it with golden glints as they ruffled lightly with the breeze coming from large, hand-held *pankhas* that were being fanned in graceful sweeps by the handmaidens.

As the sound of conch shells being blown by the priests reverberated through the hall to the chanting of 'Om Shanti, Shanti, Shanti, Om' signifying the successful completion of the yajna, King Bhima and Queen Charumati rose from their thrones to come forward and make the final offerings in the sacrificial fires. Then the golden curtains were drawn aside and Princess Damayanti stepped forward escorted by her friends. She bent down to touch the feet of Brahmarishi Damana who, placing his hand over her head, gave his blessings saying, 'May you today find the husband of your choice who will love and honour you throughout your life.'

To a flourish of trumpets, King Bhima announced the start of the swayamvara. As the kings and princes rose from their ornate thrones, Queen Charumati picked up the ceremonial garland from a large, decorative silver *thaal* and placed it in the hands of Damayanti. Chitra took the thaal, which also contained vermilion powder and turmeric paste from the Queen's hands and moved forward alongside Damayanti.

'I'm feeling so nervous and jittery,' the Princess whispered. Dressed in a white and gold ensemble, which was set off by sparkling gold and diamond jewellery, Damayanti looked so ravishingly lovely that even the gods above, and the four who had descended on earth from Indralok, could not take their eyes off who were her.

'Nonsense… it is those kings and princes lined up there who should be feeling nervous. See… some of them have already broken out into a sweat. That one there is already mopping his brow, and the Kuru prince there has an attack of wobbly knees…' Chitra sniggered as she whispered back.

'Hush-hh, don't stare Chitra… but, I cannot spot Prince Nal… oh, why did they all have to dance attendance at my father's invitation!'

Slowly, gracefully, the Princess and her train of handmaidens moved down the row. The Prince of Kamboja craned his neck forward, but Damayanti passed by without sparing a glance in his direction. She was looking out for just one face… the face of Nal. She felt Chitra's elbow digging into her side. She looked. *Oh there he was!*

But what was this? Her heart started thumping wildly and she suddenly felt dizzy. The hall seemed to tilt and sway. Her vision appeared to blur. Beads of sweat broke out on her brow.

Oh God! What is happening to me? she panicked. *Instead of one Prince Nal, I am seeing five of them standing here!*

Equally alarmed and taken aback at seeing Damayanti stagger, Chitra quickly took the garland from her hands before it could fall to the floor, and passed the thaal she was holding to one of the handmaidens and slid an arm around her waist to steady the princess.

'Hold up… come on, come on… take a deep breath Damayanti,' Chitra hissed into her ear. 'This is no time to faint and falter,' she whispered. Then turning quickly to the handmaidens escorting Damayanti, she ordered Kamakhya to quickly fetch a bowl of rosewater, and another to get a cooling drink of lemon and honey.

Damayanti's mother got up from her throne and rushed to where the hubbub had occurred. 'What's wrong? What happened?' she asked Chitra. Turning to Damayanti, she asked anxiously, 'Why have you stopped half-way, daughter?'

Turning to the Queen Mother, Chitra calmed her by saying, 'Nothing, nothing is the matter... the Princess just felt faint. It's the heat. She will be alright.'

Queen Charumati turned to the gathering of kings and princes. 'Please... please... pray be seated. The Princess is quite overwhelmed and will take a short break... we apologise for the interruption... the swayamvara will proceed soon.'

Everyone seemed to be talking at once in murmurs and whispers. The King of Kashi came up to Queen Charumati and said, 'Please... please, let the Princess rest a while... we all understand this is a long drawn out ceremonial occasion... and it could take a toll on the delicate and fair Princess. I speak on behalf of all of us gathered here... we are content to wait awhile.'

Damayanti, regaining her poise, was escorted behind the veiled curtain and made to rest on a couch. The gathering appeared to settle down as liveried attendants bearing large platters of refreshments and goblets of cool, refreshing drinks, began offering them to the honoured guests.

The little drama played out by Indra, Agni, Varuna and Yama had totally escaped everyone's notice. Upon seeing the startled look on Damayanti's face they had been secretly delighted at their own inventiveness and the smirk only left their faces once she had left. They had then instantly reverted to their original forms and sat back to wait it out like the rest of the hopefuls gathered at the swayamvara.

Despairing and despondent, Nal had all along been standing with his head down and eyes glued to the floor. So, the real cause of all the disturbance had gone unnoticed by him.

Recovering from her shock and confusion, Damayanti realised that the gods had connived to trick her into garlanding one of them, and that they were bound to resort to the same ploy once she returned to proceed with the swayamvara. How would she be able to distinguish between the five Nals, who was the *real* Prince Nal? She prayed to the gods above that they would send her some sign by which she would be able to recognise her beloved from the impostors. Just then, the trumpeters blew a second flourish to herald her re-entry. Refreshed, calm and composed, Damayanti emerged from behind the golden veil and, once again, a collective gasp went up at the sight of her radiant beauty. Smiling, she glided gracefully down the aisle accompanied by Chitra and her train of handmaidens.

While earlier the gods had observed that Prince Nal had stood a little away from them in the hope that the Princess would thus be able to identify him, this time around to avoid any such carelessness on their part, they made certain that he was more or less hemmed in by them at either end. As Damayanti stopped briefly before each contestant, he would step forward and announce his name and the kingdom he came from. When she came to pause before the next prince in line, he stepped forward saying, 'I am Prince Nal of Nishadha.'

Damayanti raise her head and shot a quick glance. *Yes, here he was, here stood her Prince Nal*, but as quickly as the thought had arisen, it vanished just as fast as another prince also stepped forward and said, 'I am Prince Nal of Nishadha.' Soon she found herself in the presence of five Nal look-alikes. She looked at each one intently, raised her hands holding the floral garland as if to drape it around his neck, then faltered and lowered it as she approached the next lookalike. The four gods had accomplished a rare work of art one could say in duplicating the features, the clothing, the regal bearing of the original Prince Nal, right down to the upward twirl of his stylish moustache. All the while, Damayanti had been searching for those distinguishing marks she had heard about that distinguished gods from their human counterparts. Yet she had not been able to discern even one of those distinguishing signs in the five handsome forms that stood smiling before her, each one with an expectant look in his eyes. She had half expected that the gods would have been overconfident of themselves and thus forgotten to conceal these distinguishing marks, but no, they had considered everything and taken care not to reveal any sign by which she could tell who was god and who was human. In such a situation, Damayanti thought her best chances lay in appealing to the nobler, more gracious side of the gods.

Folding both her hands in obeisance and in greeting, she addressed them by name and said: 'My parents, my people, indeed the very princes and kings of this great land, who are gathered here today, thank you for descending from Indralok and blessing this earth and its inhabitants with your godly presence. I am more blessed that you have chosen this auspicious occasion of my swayamvara to grace our city Kundina.'

'What on earth is this Princess up to?' wondered the four gods in the guise of Prince Nal, while Nal himself remained clueless of Damayanti's intent.

'All the Lords gathered here know that I, born of a boon given by Brahmarishi Damana to my parents, have always honoured the gods and goddesses with my devoted worship as instructed by our scriptures. It is God Almighty, who predetermines the course of life of every human being. So also, I believe, has He determined mine.

'I also believe the divine messenger who came to me in the form of a golden-winged swan and spoke in human tongue, was part of His plan to attract me towards the attributes of Prince Nal, a prince among men, whom He had chosen as the most suitable life partner for me.

'Therefore, by this truth, I appeal to you O Lords of Indralok to reveal my ordained Lord Nal to me.

'Because I stand pledged to Lord Nal also by my own vow, I plead with you to reveal my Lord to me.

'Since, in my heart and soul, I have already accepted him as my husband, so reveal him to me.

'I beseech each of you, O Lords of Indralok and Protectors of the World, to reveal your divine form, so I may discern the one who is meant to be wed to me.'

Having thus prayed to the four gods, Damayanti stood before them with hands folded, eyes lowered, and head bowed in all humility.

The four gods, each moved by her ardent plea, impressed by her firm resolve, and obeying a decree from High above – stood revealed in their divine form before Damayanti.

They stood unblinking, their skin unmoistened by sweat, their garlands in full bloom, their feet not touching the ground.

And there stood Prince Nal, blinking in astonishment, his forehead beaded with sweat, his garland showing signs of having withered, and with his feet firmly planted on the ground.

Damayanti couldn't believe her eyes as they kept darting from the gods to Nal. She was overjoyed.

A robust cheer resounded from the gathered assembly. Damayanti bent to touch the feet of each of the four gods and receive their blessings that they generously gave with both hands raised.

Indra, the Lord of all gods in Indralok, said, 'There stands your true Lord, Prince Nal of Nishadha. Go to him and garland him with your varmala which we have kept fragrant and dew-fresh just for this moment.'

Chitra came forward with the silver platter containing the garland with its flowers in glorious bloom. The fragrance that arose drifted across the hall and made Nal swoon as he lowered his head to accept the garland that Damayanti, with a fluttering heart and eyes brimming with joy, draped around his neck.

A roll of drums and a flare of trumpets marked the high point of the proceedings. The gods in heaven, and the gods attending the swayamvara, showered rose petals on the newly betrothed couple. Nal and Damayanti were then escorted to the *mandap* – the flower bedecked pavilion, where their marriage was to be solemnised according to Vedic rites. Lord Agni caused the fire to burn brighter with flames that leapt up to the skies with a merry crackle as the ghee and spices were offered to it. After Nal and Damayanti had taken the seven ceremonial rounds of the fire, they first sought and received the blessings from the four gods.

Lord Indra granted Nal the boon that the Prince would be able to behold his own godship in sacrifices and be blessed with legions thereafter. Lord Agni gave him the boon that whenever Nal desired his presence he would come to his bidding. Lord Varuna too, following Agni's example, granted a similar boon. Last, but not the least, Lord Yama granted him the boon of developing a rare skill in preparing exotic food, as well as pre-eminence in truth and virtue.

Then having bestowed their blessings for a happy wedded life, the celestials took their leave of the newly-weds.

After the customary celebrations, banquets and feasting that went on for several days, the kings and princes who had attended the swayamvara, also took leave to return to their respective kingdoms. While King Bhima and Queen Charumati would have liked to have Damayanti and Nal stay longer with them and were loath to see them go, they finally bid their farewells to the couple.

Damayanti's brothers accompanied the couple to the borders of their kingdom, while a battalion of the King's guard was deputed to escort them to the kingdom of Nishadha.

Chapter 14

RETURN TO GIRIPRASTHA

From a distance, the city appeared to be bathed in a bright golden glow. It was only when they neared its gates did Nal and Damayanti see that every house had been decorated with streamers made of marigolds in varying shades of orange – bright and pale yellow. Men, women and children were out in the streets wearing garments of the same hue. As the chariot bearing the Crown Prince Nal and his bride rolled into sight, the crowds burst into a robust cheer – the women showered fistfuls of marigold petals from the rooftops on the bridal couple and children danced in the streets to the lively beat of drums as the entourage neared the palace gates, which swung wide open to allow the chariots to pass through. Shouts of *'Rajkumar Nal ki jai, Rajkumari Damayanti ki jai'* rent the air as King Virasena, Queen Vasumati, and Pushkar came down the marbled steps of the stately palace to greet the newly-weds. Nal stepped down from the chariot and turned to hold out his hand for Damayanti to alight. While King Virasena beamed with pride, Pushkar stood wonderstruck at Damayanti's beauty and felt a stab of envy at his brother's good fortune on having won her as his bride.

Now the Queen Mother stepped forward and performed the *aarti* to welcome them. As Damayanti stepped over the threshold to tip over the copper vessel filled to the brim with rice, the traditional rite signifying fertility and prosperity, everyone applauded and handmaidens showered rose petals on the couple. Nal and Damayanti bowed low to touch the feet of King Virasena and Queen Vasumati and receive their blessings for a happy married life. The cheers rose to a deafening crescendo as the King and Queen showered silver coins over the heads of the assembled crowd. Children darted hither and thither to collect the coins as they fell tinkling onto the cobbled pathways.

Nal was grateful that the wedding feast and celebrations would only take place on the following day. Both he and Damayanti were tired and fatigued after several days spent on the road and wanted nothing more than to rest for now. So after the formalities had been over and done with, Damayanti was escorted by the Queen and her designated handmaidens to the bridal chamber that had been specially prepared for the Princess. Meanwhile, Nal was accompanied by his brother Pushkar and his dear friend Rudra to his private chambers so he could bathe, rest and be refreshed for the night when he would enter Damayanti's bridal chamber.

'So, I heard that the swayamvara developed into quite a circus of sorts,' asked Pushkar, as Nal collapsed onto a couch.

'Don't ask!' sighed Nal. 'It was quite something altogether, but I just don't have the energy to go into all that now with you and Rudra. I'll tell you all about it, another time…'

'Yes, I can see that… don't stress yourself…' said Rudra, handing him a goblet of wine. 'Here, drink this… while I arrange a masseur to ease the fatigue from your body after the long, ragged ride you've just survived. The roads are not in great shape, I know. Besides you only have a couple of hours to rest before you grace the bridal chamber tonight.'

'Well… all's well that ends well, I suppose,' commented Pushkar with a long drawn out sigh.

'I will be back in a couple of hours Nal, after you have rested and slept awhile. You won't be getting much sleep later this night,' winked Rudra. Turning to Pushkar, he said, 'Come, we will while away the time by playing a few rounds of dice.'

Nal hurled a cushion at Rudra's retreating back. 'Get lost, you idiot!'

'Don't keep the Princess waiting!' Rudra cheekily added as his parting shot.

Meanwhile the gods who had tarried for some days on earth to take in the sights and sounds were planning to leave for swargalok after they had rested for the night in a sylvan glade.

'I am really tired!' Varuna exclaimed as he yawned and stretched his limbs.

'So am I, after all that masquerading and posturing at Damayanti's swayamvara,' echoed Varuna. 'Whose idea was it, anyway, to resort to this charade?'

'Stop grumbling... we've all enjoyed the mischief we've been up to,' laughed Indra. 'Don't pretend you all didn't have fun... Right, Yama?'

'Well... I admit to being rather jealous of Nal's physique,' remarked Agni. 'But I have to admire the way he conducted himself in this entire situation. Which is why I gave him the boon of my assistance, if and when he were ever to need it.'

'All's well that ends well, I say... and I for one wish Nal and Damayanti a happy married life,' concluded Yama. 'Now let's get some rest before we ascend to heaven at daybreak.'

'Look at our heaven in the night sky. Doesn't it really look beautiful when seen from Earth?' Indra sighed, lying down with his arms crossed behind his head. 'I can't wait to get back.'

When he got no response, he turned his head to look at the others and saw they were fast asleep. The clamour of crickets had faded away. Glow worms twinkled in the trees and bushes. A stillness had gradually fallen over the forest glade enveloped now in the cloak of night.

It was much later that Varuna who was roused from his sleep as he felt a hand shaking his shoulder and someone telling him, 'Get up, get up!' Rubbing his eyes, Varuna mumbled, 'Go away, let me sleep!'

'Get up, get up!' the voice kept insisting.

Varuna opened his eyes to see that it was the asura Kali, accompanied by another asura Dwapara, who was rousing him.

'What's the matter with you… what are both of you doing here?' Varuna asked, perplexed at the new arrivals.

'We are going for Damayanti's swayamvara which is to be held today. One of us hopes to win her as his bride,' Kali said.

Varuna laughed so loudly that he woke up the other gods. 'What's so funny Varuna, why are you laughing like a mad man... er... sorry god!'

'Look at these two stupid asuras,' he said pointing to Kali and Dwapara. 'They are all dressed up to go to Damayanti's swayamvara! These dolts don't even know which day it is!'

Indra smirked. 'Asuras will always remain the ignoramuses… they seem to have no idea of the passage of time. Don't you know that the swayamvara was held some days ago? She has already been wedded to Prince Nal of Nishadha!'

Hearing this, Kali was livid with anger. His face turned a dark purple, his eyes nearly popped out and the veins in his forehead throbbed. He stomped the ground with his huge feet and bellowed, 'How dare she wed Nal! How dare she! I will teach both of them a lesson they will never forget! I will ruin this marriage, come hell or high water! Just you wait and see!'

'Calm down Kali, get a hold on yourself… you mad Asura!' commanded Agni. 'What's done is done… and both Nal and Damayanti have our blessings and our protection from now on.'

'Huh! Your protection and your blessings! I will see what good they are… they are nothing!' Kali retorted. 'The *Shani dasha*[1] has begun in Nal's life and I am going to take full advantage of this. You don't know the extent of the wickedness I can go to. I will make both their lives a living hell!'

[1] The astrological period when the planet Saturn, usually considered a malefic influence in a horoscope, enters a person's life for a period of seven-and-a-half years.

Varuna in the hope that he could pour oil over troubled waters sought to placate Kali. 'Get a hold of yourself Kali. What is done, is done. Show some grace in the matter. Let them both live in peace. Go back to your Asura kingdom and choose one of your own kind. You are not fit to even touch Damayanti's little toe, nor can you match Prince Nal in any way!'

Dwarapa angrily stepped forward at hearing this insult to his friend. 'You gods think no end of yourselves ever since you stole from us the vessel containing amrita that was churned from the ocean. Just because you are immortal doesn't give you any right to feel superior.'

'We will see who will stop us from ruining the married bliss of Nal and Damayanti! In fact, I will put my plan into action this very day!' fumed Kali.

'Fine!' Indra said acidly. 'You do what you can, and we will do everything in our power to foil your plans. Now get lost, the both of you!'

Chapter 15

One Misstep

Twelve years had passed since King Virasena had passed away. Twelve eventful years which had seen the ascension of Nal to the throne of the Nishadha kingdom, his having performed the *ashwamedha* or horse sacrifice to establish his suzerainty and be honoured with the title of *Chakravartin*, akin to an emperor. The kingdom had expanded and prospered. Pushkar had been given a region somewhere in the eastern region of Nishadha to govern but he was none too happy at being away from the centre of power. Damayanti had borne a son named Indrasen, and a daughter named Indraseni, and had ensured the continuance of the dynasty of Nal and his forefathers.

Twelve years had passed since the day Kali, along with Dwapara, in the guise of ordinary menials, had entered into the service of Nal at Giriprastha. Over time, the shrewd Kali had wormed his way into being posted as one of Nal's personal attendants so he could observe Nal at close quarters, studying his likes and dislikes. He knew what time he woke, what time he slept. All these years, he waited patiently for the day Nal would make one move, one slip, however insignificant, and one which Kali could use against him to plot Nal's downfall and turn the tide of fortune against him. That day was now about to dawn and one careless misstep was all it would take to spell disaster and doom.

After answering the call of nature one day, Nal, in his haste not to miss the evening prayers and unmindful of the fact that he had not washed his feet prior to entering the prayer room, performed the twilight prayer. Seeing Nal thus defiling the sanctity and ritual of prayer, Kali seized the moment. Even though Nal had unwittingly committed this breach, he had given Kali the opening he had been waiting for all these years. It gave him an opening to immediately enter Nal and bewitch his mind. As Kali entered his body, Nal, unaware of what had just happened, felt a sudden spasm jolt his body. He somehow managed to complete worshipping the deities. Then, feeling a splitting headache coming on, he sent for Rudra and then went and laid down thinking that his feeling of intense discomfort would soon pass. Seeing the uncomfortable state Nal was in, Rudra asked an attendant to go notify Queen Damayanti, who came rushing.

'What's the matter… what has happened?' an alarmed Damayanti asked, as she put a hand on Nal's forehead. 'By Varuna! Your forehead is burning!' she exclaimed. 'Have you been out in the sun all day… you seem to have a touch of the fever!' She turned to her maid and asked her to fetch a bowl of rose water.

'No… no, I was feeling fine all day…' murmured Nal. 'When I entered the prayer room, I suddenly had a spell of dizziness and began sweating profusely. Then suddenly my body went cold and I just about made it to my chamber with the help of an attendant.'

While Damayanti was putting a cold compress dipped in rose water on Nal's forehead, she asked Rudra to get a mild opiate from the royal physician. 'Here, drink this,' she said raising the goblet to his lips. 'It will help ease the headache and you will feel better after a good sleep.' Getting up from his bedside, she went and drew the curtains across the windows and quietly signalled everyone to leave the room. She then sat on a stool by Nal's bed and picking up a fan made of sun-dried bamboo stalks, began to gently wave it over him as he drifted off to sleep.

The transformation when it came was so gradual that no one, least of all Nal himself, even noticed. And, of course, the wife is always the last one to know what is amiss. Among the first signs that became discernible were a lessening interest towards matters of State. It had been observed that grievances of the common folk that were usually addressed by Nal in an open court every day were getting short shrift. Another daily practice of inspecting the army parade in the mornings had almost ceased. King Nal was now given to carousing with cronies and surrounded by 'yes' men. Still, these could have been passed off as temporary diversions, but what did not go down well with his senior advisers was their monarch's new-found fascination with the game of dice. What had earlier been just an occasional pastime, and one in which he excelled, had now become an obsession and an addiction. When Damayanti came to know of this, she shrugged it off as a passing fancy. *After all*, she reasoned, *Nal does need to unwind and relax after a long day attending to various matters of the court and the kingdom*. But at the back of her mind, the thought that somewhere, somehow, something was not right continued to niggle.

Yet, two people were very happy with the way events had recently turned out to their advantage. Kali and Dwapara could barely contain their excitement and it was this small victory that encouraged Kali to implement the next step of his devious plan to wreak vengeance on Nal. He now impressed upon Dwapara the need to move fast and prevailed upon him to journey to Pushkar's palace and watch for an opportunity when he could subvert Pushkar by entering his body and poisoning his mind towards Nal. Idle minds are the devil's playground and these two demons were the very personification of evil.

The festival of Navratri – the nine nights dedicated to the worship of goddess Durga had culminated in burning an effigy of Ravana to signify the victory of good over evil. Diwali was just a few weeks away and on Damayanti's urging, Nal had agreed to take a short break from his kingly duties and pay a visit to Pushkar. The two brothers hadn't met for quite some time now and, aware that they had grown apart, she had waited for an opportune moment to suggest such a trip. She had also reasoned that it would provide not only her and their two children a welcome break but help Nal spend more time with them, once he was away from Giriprastha. And so the royal entourage set out for Pushkar's palace in the eastern plains of Nishadha.

Pushkar had spared no effort to give his brother's family a royal welcome and went out of his way to charm and win over both his nephew and niece Indrasen and Indraseni. If Nal found all this somewhat of a put on, fully aware of his brother's innate nature which was resentful to a point and self-serving, he kept his opinion to himself. But he did, in a private moment, remark to Damayanti that this was not the Pushkar he knew. 'Something about his behaviour just does not ring true!' he mused, but his wife told him was just being a bit over critical. 'With time people do change, and he seems to have changed for the better,' she averred. 'So stop thinking about all this, and let us all enjoy our stay here.'

One fine morning while Pushkar was showing his brother and Damayanti around the stables that housed his breeds of cows and horses, Nal saw a magnificent white bull grazing in the field. The creature raised its head towards them both – defiant and proud. 'He is stunning!' remarked Nal. 'What musculature! What bearing!'

'Indeed! He has sired several prize calves!' Pushkar boasted with pride.

'I can't take my eyes off him, Pushkar! Do you see the way he is looking at me! Oh, you must gift him to me, dear brother!' Nal exclaimed with rising excitement.

'Ha! That I cannot do. What will become of the breeding programme I have for him. No, no… I am sorry Nal, I cannot part with him. He is almost worth a king's ransom!'

Kali, who unknown to Nal, was egging him on, made him plead: 'Come on Pushkar, my heart is set on him. Have I asked anything of you before this? Please don't refuse my request!'

Pushkar hemmed and hawed and while he was mulling over it, Dwapara twisted his mind to make him utter the words that would spell impending doom and disaster.

'Okay, but on one condition, brother!' Pushkar had a new set to his chin. 'Let us play at dice for the white bull, if your heart is set on having him. If I lose, he is yours!' he exclaimed.

Although Nal sensed there was a challenge couched in his invitation, and that too given in the presence of Damayanti, there was no way he could possibly refuse. He smiled, 'And what do you want in exchange, if you win Pushkar?'

'We'll see to that later Nal, as the game progresses... don't worry! But you will have to be prepared to give whatever I ask for!' Pushkar replied. Damayanti could have sworn that a sneer had fleetingly crossed his face. Had it? Her heart had skipped a beat, but then she dismissed the thought. She had probably just imagined it.

'Of course, Pushkar! You have my word!' Nal said fondly.

'Come brother,' Pushkar smiled amiably throwing an arm across Nal's shoulders. 'The evening is still young, let us have a practice game, shall we? We haven't played together since years and I, at least, am sure I must have lost my touch!' Then turning to Damayanti, he made a small bow and asked, 'Won't you also join us?'

'Thank you Pushkar, although I would have loved to watch you two brothers play, but I must decline... it's the children's hour and they must be waiting for me. You two go on right ahead.'

'I won't be long, Damayanti,' assured Nal. 'I will come before the children are put to bed to tuck them in.'

Smiling, Damayanti said fondly, 'It's okay Nal... brothers need to bond together and I hope you both use this time to come closer.'

Chapter 16

The Die Is Cast

From her window, Damayanti was watching her children at play when much to her surprise she saw dark clouds gathering in the evening sky. A sudden gust of wind lashed the drapes across her face. The sight of this unusual occurrence at this time of year made her call out to the children to come in, but her voice did not carry as the wind swept it away. As the wind picked up speed she saw clusters of leaves being whipped around and up into the air.

Alarmed, she ran out into the garden and shielding the children under her robe hustled them indoors. Hours later, awake besides a sleeping Nal, Damayanti could not help but think… *It's an ill omen that bodes no good.*

The wind howled and the storm raged all night. But out in the storm, Kali and Dwapara cackled and rubbed their hands in glee. 'Did you manage to get hold of the dice that are going to be used in the game of *chausar* tomorrow?' asked Kali.

Dwapara pulled out a bag and rattled it near Kali's ear. 'What do you think these are? While Pushkar was away, I managed to smuggle it out of his private chamber.' Shoving his hand inside the cloth bag, he pulled out *Vrisha* – the principal dice that would determine which way the game went. 'Isn't she a beauty, Kali! The *vibhitaka*[1] nut it is made from has been delicately carved and gilded with copper.'

'Hmmm… indeed! The other two are quite exquisite, too!' Kali said, admiring the handiwork. 'Now here is the plan, Dwapara. Listen carefully, because we cannot afford to bungle things up tomorrow when the game starts. I am keeping the principal dice with me, while the cowries stay with you for tonight.'

'What for, Kali? I must return them to Pushkar's cabinet before he misses them tomorrow!'

'I have to cast some spells on it. Don't worry, well before the game of chausar is due to start I will give it to you for by then my spirit will have entered the principal dice. Every time Nal makes his throw, I will be controlling the roll of the dice and make sure that it comes up as a 'no-win'.

'But what is going to be my role in all of this, Kali?' asked a perplexed Dwapara.

'You, my dear friend, are going to work on Pushkar's avaricious, grasping nature. This game is not going to end in one day. I can bet that it will go on for several weeks, fuelled by his greed for more… and more.'

Dwapara's eyes shone with malicious glee. 'You are brilliant, Kali. They have rightly named the worst throw of the dice – Kali – after you! And now I also know why the fourth yuga, the Kali yuga, is so named too!'

'Not just that Dwapara, the four throws of the dice are all named after the four yugas – *Krita* (Satya), *Devita* (Dwapara), *Trita* (Treta), and *Kali*. And you know the last, the Kali yuga, the one over which I preside is the worst of the lot!

'Be that as it may. Let's get to it then. I must rush now and

1 The nuts of the tree are rounded but with five flatter sides. It seems to be these nuts are used as dice in the epic poem Mahabharata. A handful of nuts would be cast on a gaming board and the players would have to call whether an odd or even number of nuts had been thrown. In the Nalopakhyana Parva , King Rituparna demonstrates his ability to count large numbers instantaneously by counting the number of nuts on an entire bough.

replace these dice before Pushkar starts missing them. I will see you tomorrow before the game begins.'

The lull after the storm, that had raged all night, was just as disquieting. A heavy, almost deathly, silence hung in the air that made Damayanti feel even more uneasy than the fury of the storm that had preceded it. Deep within, she had for some time now felt that Nal was not his earlier self… why, even the children had sensed it! Indraseni had only a few days ago asked her, 'What is wrong with Father?' Although on the surface he appeared to be his usual self, she knew there were undercurrents rippling beneath. She had readily agreed to this visit to Pushkar's kingdom in the hope that the brothers would reconcile their differences, and that seemed to be working. 'But… but…' the furrows on her forehead deepened.

'What are you thinking of Damayanti?' asked Nal, coming out of his bath. 'Come on, cheer up, the storm has passed and the sun is shining. Come… let me see the radiance of your smile,' he cajoled. 'How do I look? Imagine playing dice for a white Brahmin Bull! What must have I been thinking!' he laughed out loud. 'Come now, it is time we went to the gaming chamber of our dear Pushkar. He and his cronies will be waiting for us while I will have only you by my side, although you will be sitting behind a veiled curtain with the other ladies.'

'Haven't I always been by your side since the day of our marriage? Here, let me put the tilak on your forehead before we leave!'

As they entered the hall where the game was to be held, Pushkar came forward accompanied by his wife. 'Aha… there you are my dear brother. Come, come… let's be seated… my palm is already itching to feel the texture of the dice!' Turning towards an aide, he commanded: 'Bring us the box containing the dice!' Then turning again toward Nal, he said: 'Your reputation as an expert dice player has spread far and wide, dear brother. You have all the time in the world now to play… you are the Chakravartin king, sovereign ruler of all! And you have earned all the fame and glory that is being heaped upon you! So, as my sovereign Lord you have the privilege of having the first throw of the dice.'

'Come, come Pushkar… this is just a game between two brothers. We are not fighting for kingdoms nor an empire! It's a friendly game… and the prize? A white bull I had admired and whom you staked rather than simply gifting to me. But you have always wanted to fight over the smallest things ever since you were a child,' smiled Nal.

'I had to fight for everything, even for our father's attention who doted only on you … his fair, handsome and accomplished son who could do no wrong. I was always the black sheep in his eyes,' Pushkar laughed, although there was an edge to his laughter.

'Oh no, anyway, our mother loved you more because you were the youngest!' countered Nal. 'So it all evened out, Pushkar. Come, let the game begin!'

Palming an intricately carved ivory cylinder, Nal rattled the dice in it before letting it roll on to the colourful square of cloth known as the *chauras* whose four strips extended north, south, east and westwards. Nal moved his cowries three places on the chausar. 'Poor throw,' he muttered. 'Your turn, brother,' he said handing the ivory cylinder to Pushkar.

As Pushkar palmed the ivory cylinder and got ready to cast the dice, Dwapara, who had entered the second dice of the pair, guided it such that it came face up on a higher number. Pushkar rubbed his hands in glee. As the dice were cast again and again, Nal, except for a few reasonably decent throws, was seen to be not in his best element, whereas his brother, on the other hand, appeared to having an amazing run of good luck. At the end of the day, the game had gone in Pushkar's favour. Nal asked Pushkar 'So, what do you want for having bested me at the game today?'

'How about giving up the hoard of gold and silver from your treasury?' smirked Pushkar. 'But I am a fair man, so if you like you can win it all back by another round of the game tomorrow!'

Thus, the game that had begun almost in jest and as a friendly match, acquired overtones of avarice and bitter rivalry over the succeeding days as Kali kept subverting Nal's mind and goading him on to win back all that had lost – gold, silver, precious stones to chariots, horses and his prized elephants.

'Brother,' Nal said one day after the game kept dragging on as his losses kept mounting. Let us move back to Giriprastha and continue our game. I have been away longer than I had intended to, and as King I must also attend to some matters of State.'

This is exactly what Pushkar also wanted and he fell in readily with his brother's suggestion. And so the royal entourage moved to Giriprastha.

Now all that was left for Nal to wager was his throne along with the kingdom. When the citizens got wind of this, they gathered outside the council hall waiting for an audience with King Nal to get him to desist from playing any further and gambling the kingdom away. But Nal, far too absorbed in planning his strategy and getting ready to go for the day's game, refused to entertain them. Seeing this, the crowd led by the chief councillors of the city went to plead before Damayanti.

When Damayanti was informed by the chief councillors that their king was preparing to wager his throne in the day's game, she visibly paled and felt sick to the pit of her stomach. 'Gracious lady,' said the elder of the councillors, 'this is no time to pander to the king's whim. We beg of you to go to him immediately before he sits down at the game and make him desist from any further foolhardiness.'

'Perhaps it would be wiser for you all to approach the Queen Mother, Vasumati, as my revered father-in-law King Virasena is out on a diplomatic mission. The only person who may be able to dissuade Nal would he his mother,' suggested Damayanti. However, Vasumati, who had never been an assertive woman, expressed her helplessness in the way the events appeared to be playing out. 'My sons are grown men. Pushkar has always been envious of Nal's superior prowess in almost every sphere of life, and secretly nursed a deep grudge against him. Now that he seems to be gaining an upper hand, he will never let go of the opportunity to maximise his advantatge. I am afraid neither of my sons is willing to listen to any reason at this point time. Yes, if their father had been here, perhaps he may have been able to avert the disaster that appears to be looming before us.' Dabbing away the tears in her eyes, Vasumati, her head bowed down in despair, excused herself from the gathering of the councillors. The way the game had been steadily going from bad to worse for Nal over the past many days was a sign that even Damayanti had begun to dread. Although the portents boded doom, in her heart of hearts she still had her faith pinned on Nal's strategising and masterful play, which could somehow in one stroke win back all that he had so far lost to Pushkar. But, once he wagered his throne, there would be nothing left to recover. So, trembling with an inner rage mixed with fear of the consequences should the game go badly again for her husband, Damayanti rushed out to confront him before he entered the chamber where the game was about to begin.

'Nal!' she exclaimed catching him just as he was about to enter the chamber. 'Your chief councillors along with some prominent citizens have been waiting for an audience with you. Don't you even care to hear what they have to say? They have heard that you are going to wager your throne at the game today! How can you be so blind and foolish, Nal! What on earth has possessed you that you are unmindful of any advice, in your foolhardy pursuit of a game in which it is clear to everyone that you are hopelessly being outsmarted and outwitted? Can you really be so blind that you cannot see the yawning pit you are falling into?

'Don't interfere in something that is between two brothers, Damayanti. Go back to your chambers!' is all Nal said.

When Damayanti went back to the councillors with despair

written all over her face, she addressed them saying, 'I fear for him and I fear for our kingdom and its people. He will not listen to anyone and is determined to have his own way.'

Upon hearing this, the grieved and dejected councillors and citizens hung their heads in shame. There was nothing they could do but return to their homes. Damayanti, with a thudding heart, retired to her bedchamber, unable to witness another humiliating defeat of Nal at the hands of his brother.

In what was to be the last and final game, Kali used all his might to counter Nal's deft throw of the dice and at the last second caused his wrist to spasm and twitch. The dice landed face up with two snake eyes, the worst throw ever, staring at Nal who was devastated.

Pushkar was elated. He had won, he had won all that Nal had owned and ruled over. But there was still one prize left that he coveted. So he addressed a dejected Nal, 'What now brother? You have lost everything. You don't even own the robes and jewels you are wearing! But there is still one more thing you own. Come, are you willing to stake Damayanti in the final game? If perchance you were to win, I will still return everything I have won. But...'

The Queen Mother paled and felt faint when she heard of the final stake that had been proposed by Pushkar. Shocked and rendered almost immobile, she could not even utter a word of protest.

Nal, finding some remnant of self-respect within himself, stared at Pushkar. Eyes blazing, he bellowed, 'Don't you even dare harbour any thought of possessing Damayanti! You are welcome to all you have won from me – my treasure, my armies, my kingdom... but I will not stand cursed in my own eyes were I to do what you so shamefully suggest!'

'So be it!' sneered Pushkar. 'Hand over your kingly robes, jewels and crown to my servant here. Summon your wife in my presence. She too will have to go without all these creature comforts now. As of now, both of you stand banished from Giriprastha. You are to leave with nothing but a simple peasants' garment on your backs.'

The silence in the hall was palpable. Everyone had their eyes downcast and could not look their king Nal in the eye. As Nal began to remove his royal robes and jewels, a jeering Pushkar threw a loose garment of sackcloth at his brother's feet.

'All is lost, my Queen!' Vrihatsena, the children's nurse, came rushing in to break the news to Damayanti. Turning a sorrowful look at the nurse, she said: 'This is not the time to mourn over what is lost, Vrihatsena. Rush to the charioteer Varshaneya, tell him to harness the finest and sturdiest steeds of the King to his chariot and meet me at the western gate of the palace. We have no time to waste and every minute, every second, counts.'

As soon as Varshaneya rode up in his chariot drawn by two steeds to the gate, he found Damayanti standing with her two children. She said, 'Varshaneya, just as the king has always reposed his full trust in you, so have I all these years. Even as I speak, your king must be handing over his crown to Pushkar. Our fate, which has been in the doldrums for the past few months, has been sealed. I have been summoned to present myself before Pushkar. But before I go, I must ask you for a favour.'

'Your every wish is my command, fair Queen… what would you have me do?'

'I have packed the belongings of my children Indrasen and Indraseni. Without wasting any more time, I entrust them in your care. You are to immediately take them in your chariot and ride full speed to my father's palace at Kundina. They will be safe there.' Then quickly turning to embrace her son and daughter, she said, 'Go with Varshaneya. You will stay in your grandfather's house until I come for you.'

Just then, dragging her feet as if they were weighed down by shackles, Vasumati came in escorted by her handmaiden. 'Damayanti, let the children stay with me. I will look after them and they will be safe here.'

Damayanti was firm. 'No, dear Mother... Pushkar's intentions are all too clear. He wants to be the sovereign and will not allow anything to stand in his way to the throne. The life of my children, and especially that of Indrasen, will always be a thorn in the flesh of Pushkar and he will one day feel compelled to remove Indrasen out of his way. My children are not safe here!'

'But mother, why can't we stay here with you even if father has lost his kingdom?' asked Indrasen.

'I have no answer for you right now, son! Your father and I have both been banished from the kingdom, and I must go where your father goes. Just do as I tell you,' Damayanti patted his head.

To Varshaneya, she said: 'Go now, before orders are sent out to secure all the gates. Take them safely to Kundina and leave the chariot and the horses there. Then, if you wish to stay there, my father King Bhima will honourably take you in his employ. But if you wish to go elsewhere, you are at liberty to go wherever you wish.'

Once the chariot carrying Vrihatsena and the children disappeared from her sight, Damayanti walked back to present herself in answer to the summons sent by Pushkar. She was aghast to see Nal in a peasant's garment standing before Pushkar who was seated on the throne.

'Come, come... Damayanti... where are your queenly airs now?' Pushkar taunted. 'Look at your husband standing here like any ordinary farmhand in a sackcloth garment, shorn of all his possessions – save one. That is You! I had made him a very generous offer of taking you into my harem. But the upright fool would not stake you in one last game.'

'He is my husband – and your elder brother, Pushkar. At least show him some respect,' requested Damayanti.

'What use is such a husband, Damayanti?' mocked Pushkar. 'Leave alone clothes, he won't even be able to provide a roof over your head now! I make you one last offer – either enter my harem and live in comfort, or be similarly banished and condemned to ignominy.'

Damayanti walked over to where her husband stood. 'My resolve and my duty is to be by my husband in whatever state he keeps me,' she answered. 'I go where Nal goes.'

'Then the even bigger fool is you!' shouted Pushkar. 'Get out of my sight. Shed your jewels and royal robes and wear what my wife has chosen for you – the single-piece cotton slip like the peasant women wear. And together get out of my kingdom. I don't want to see your miserable faces around here!'

'As you wish, Pushkar,' Turning to her husband she smiled and taking hold of his arm said: 'Come husband, let us leave. And pray, stop looking so shamefaced. This was fated to be. The city councillors and citizens are crowding the streets of Giriprastha. Even in our misfortune, let them see their king retain a semblance of dignity and composure,' she added as they stepped out of the palace and walked down the streets that were lined with men, women and children who stood with their heads bowed and eyes rooted to the ground.

In utter silence that made it all the more deafening, Nal and Damayanti, without a backward glance and staring straight ahead, walked out of the city gates.

Chapter 17

Homeless And Hopeless

No sooner had Nal and Damayanti departed from the palace did Pushkar issue a proclamation that the heralds were instructed to announce in every street square of Giriprastha.

'Hear, hear, hear ... anyone seen and caught offering food or shelter to the former King and Queen will be committing a crime against the State and will be put to instant death. Hear… hear… hear…' the message was carried loud and clear by drumbeaters throughout the city. Having heard enough tales in the past of Pushkar's temperament and treatment of those who had crossed him at some time or the other, the proclamation struck terror in the hearts of the people.

Clad in their simple peasants' garments, Nal and Damayanti arrived at nightfall on the outskirts of the city to find all doors shut against them. No one stepped out to offer a word of solace, leave alone food or shelter for the night. Beaten by cruel fate and drained by tensions of the past month, they crouched against a wall and sought succour and warmth huddled next to each other.

'In whose care have you left the children? Will they be safe from the intrigues of Pushkar?' asked Nal.

'When I realised which way the wind was blowing, I immediately sent for Varshaneya and packed them off without any further delay to my father's palace in Kundina. The children will be safe and looked after well over there,' Damayanti told him. 'We only have ourselves to worry about.'

'You must be hungry,' Nal asked hesitantly.

'Constantly worrying about you losing at the game, along with your mind, not to mention your kingdom in bits and pieces day after day, I have become accustomed to going hungry,' Damayanti said with a wan smile. 'Anyway, no one is going to offer us food here, so why even think about it?'

For three days and three nights, they lingered on the outskirts of the capital city which, apart from a few soldiers wore a mostly deserted look, with the people staying indoors. They could not bear to see the plight of their beloved King and Queen and chance upon looking them in the face or having to avert their eyes if they happened to come across them. Without anyone coming to their aid or offering even a scrap of food, leave alone offering shelter, Nal was somehow able to alleviate their hunger pangs by gathering edible leaves of some plants, berries and wild fruit that had fallen to the ground.

On the fourth day, Damayanti said: 'The city and its citizens, fearing Pushkar's retaliation, cannot and are not going to come to our aid. It is time for us to shake its very dust off our feet and go take refuge for a while in the outlying forest. At least, there you may be able to hunt some game which I can cook over a fire.' And so they set out, reaching the welcoming sanctuary of the forest as dusk was falling.

'At least here I don't feel as if a thousand eyes are peering at me all the time from behind closed doors and windows,' sighed Damayanti as they stopped to rest beside a fallen log. 'I am tired and weary… and so must you be.'

'I am solely to blame for the sorry state we have fallen into,' Nal moaned clutching his hair and shaking his head. 'By rebuffing your several pleas to come and listen to what the councillors and citizens had come to say, I showed I didn't care for what happened to you or to them – maddened with the lust for winning as I was back there.'

'When you didn't have the foresight then, what use now is

this knowledge in hindsight? Berating yourself now is neither going to ease your conscience nor improve our present situation. I am not absolving you of all blame, but this is not the time for self-flagellation. What's done, is done. Something will occur to you after you have had a restful night in this haven of peace,' counselled Damayanti.

'You are right. Anyway, I will go gather some twigs and branches to light a fire. The night is going to get a bit chilly in these garments and it will help keep us warm besides keeping us safe from wild animals, if there be any hovering around.'

Mentally and physically drained, Damayanti was fast asleep by the time Nal got the fire going. Tears welled up in Nal's eyes as he gazed at her sleeping form.

The smoke stung Nal's eyes so he began rubbing them and woke up to find Damayanti stoking the fire and roasting some edible roots she had picked in the forest, while something was brewing in an earthen pot she had found discarded near a stream flowing some distance away.

'What are you roasting?' he asked.

'These are some wild yams I was able to dig out near that tree. And I am brewing a concoction of some tulsi leaves and ginger root. At least we will be able to feed ourselves better here in the forest as out there in the city we had to go hungry,' she replied, pushing back a lock of hair that had fallen across her eyes. 'Why don't you go freshen up at the stream? This will be done by then and we can both share a meal, however frugal it may be.'

'Don't worry, my love… after that I shall go out into the forest and find us something more substantial to eat for tonight. We both need to preserve our strength and I will definitely bring home…'

Damayanti couldn't help herself and she laughed, 'The forest has already become home?'

Nal gave a sheepish smile. 'Sorry… I meant to say I will bring back a brace of partridges or wood pigeons… if not that, I will bring you some fresh fish from the stream.'

Their mood had lightened considerably by the time Nal got back and sat down to drink the energising brew from the earthen pot. Damayanti ventured, hesitantly, to voice a thought that had been niggling at her: 'Nal… why don't we go to Kundina to my father's place? He will surely welcome us with open arms…'

'No, Damayanti… I have brought this misfortune upon us… I cannot face your father with my soiled reputation and besmirched name, as a monarch who gambled away his kingdom. And what effect do you think it will have upon the children seeing their father in this sorry state? However, I do think that you can and should make your own way to Kundina to be with them.'

'I will not leave your side… not for the comforts of my father's palace… as for the children I am not worried, they will be well looked after by my parents,' she replied firmly. 'Anyway our immediate concern is to arrange for some food tonight. You said you were going to…'

'Yes-yes… I'm going to see what lies in store for me now. And please don't wander too deep into the forest while I am away,' Nal said getting up to leave.

Thinking that he would first try and see if he could capture some game, he sauntered off into the forest. Humming softly to himself, he marvelled at the pristine beauty of nature resplendent in the variety of trees and shrubs and the wild flowers hanging from boughs here and there. The chatter of monkeys above as they swung from branch to branch brought a smile to his face. He mimicked their chatter much to the astonishment of the monkeys who stopped and stared at him alarmed, before scuttling away among the trees. Nal laughed, startled for a minute at hearing his own voice, which had remained muted for almost the past month while he was engrossed in the game of dice that had played out so badly.

What had happened back there? he mused. *He was a good player; in fact, he was rather renowned for his skill and stratagems, not to mention good luck, at the game. Had his mind become addled when he had begun losing throw after throw of the dice? Or was it just that his luck had run out?* He shook his head to shrug off the thought. What use was it to think of all that now? Rethinking his moves, reliving the game was not going to change anything. If anything, he would just end up wallowing in misery and this was no time to be indulging in it. Squaring his shoulders, he walked carefully so as not to step on any twigs or dried leaves that would crack or crackle underfoot and make any untoward noise that could scare the game away.

At a little distance, he spied a pair of what appeared to be the long-tailed birds of paradise with their colourful plumes pecking away at something, probably some seeds or berries that had fallen on the ground. He froze to the spot and looked around for a branch or stone he could hurl at them so he could kill them both with one well-aimed throw. His heart plummeted as he found nothing near at hand and any hope of capturing the two, and providing Damayanti and himself with a substantially nourishing meal after many a day, seemed to vanish, when from the depth of his despair a thought surfaced. Nal didn't think twice. He drew up the garment over his head and carefully weighting it with a knot at the four corners let it fly to fall over the birds and entrap them underneath. Naked, he rushed forward to grab them but just as he was within reach the garment flew up with the birds underneath giving it wing. Nal was horrified as he looked at the fluttering cloth and stood rooted to the spot when he heard the birds cackle and mock him in a human voice:

'Oh you piteous fool, you thought that you could oppose us and not be punished for your temerity? Those other four gods let you off very easily, but I am Kali and this is Dwapara. And your life has entered the unfortunate phase of Shani dasha. Do you know what happens when one is under the influence of Shani devata? I am empowered to take over and can ruin the person if I so wish!'

Flabbergasted, Nal asked, 'But what have I ever done to offend you Kali?'

'You foiled my attempt to marry Damayanti! And she insulted us by stubbornly choosing you, a mere mortal, over us gods and asuras. When I met the gods returning from her swayamvara, I vowed to have my vengeance and wreck your marital bliss. I waited twelve years to strike!' shrieked Shani.

Nal was perplexed and confused. 'But, I lost my kingdom to my wicked brother Pushkar in a game of dice! You had nothing to do with that!'

'The more fool you were for thinking that,' put in Dwapara. 'I possessed and subverted Pushkar's mind, influencing him to invite you for the game of dice.'

'And my spirit entered Vrisha, the principal dice, and controlled how it fell despite your skill at the throw. You think Pushkar could have won otherwise? It was Dwapara who fed his vanity and ambition and I who conspired to ruin you by instigating you to wager all your wealth and your entire kingdom in the false hope that you could win the next game. I overpowered your mind and made you blind to the consequences of a game that was made to stretch out over weeks and days!' Shani boasted.

'We have had our revenge! We have humbled you, the once mighty Chakravartin king, and brought you to your knees! We leave you now without a shred of clothing to hide your nakedness – you have nothing left to cover your shame,' mocked Dwapara giving the final twist to their knife-edged words.

'You are a doomed man, and so is your beloved wife! We doubt even the boons the four gods gave you on your wedding day are ever going to be of any use to you. So we cannot even say 'Fare well!' mocked the demonic pair as they flew off with the garment and disappeared from Nal's sight.

Breaking off a creeper vine from a tree and some large peepal leaves, Nal wrapped it around his waist and tucked the peepal leaves into the belt of vine to cover his shame. Desolate and despondent, he trudged back empty-handed to where he had left Damayanti. Alarmed to see him in such a state and after listening to his tale of woe, she struck her forehead with both hands and lamented, 'Is there going to be no end to our miseries?'

Her sobs brought tears to Nal's eyes. He let her cry her heart out before putting a comforting arm around and drawing her close to his chest. He kept stroking her head till she calmed down and gently wiped the tears that were still rolling down her cheeks. 'I am afraid we shall have to go completely hungry tonight. I have not brought anything with me.'

Damayanti brushed a hand to remove the strands of hair that were clinging to her cheeks. 'No... don't worry. While you were away I found some leaves of spinach and a growth of mushrooms under a tree. It won't take me long to get a pot of broth going. Just take a look and tell me, are these mushrooms the edible kind? You have a good eye for such things. And there some fruits still left over from the morning.'

'Damayanti, I have been thinking...' Nal ventured hesitantly, not quite knowing how to put what he was going to tell her into words.

'I seem to have lost my capacity to even think these days,' she sighed, putting the clay pot on the burning coals. 'So, you were saying you have been thinking... about what?'

'You should really go to your father's house Damayanti... you don't have to suffer for my mistakes. It pains me to see you undergoing such hardship on my account. I have brought this upon myself and I alone should atone for my sins, why should you have to bear the burden?'

'I have taken seven rounds of the fire with you, whereby I also vowed to always remain by your side under all circumstances.

But I agree that we don't have to put ourselves through all these hardships. I will go if you will come with me. You know my father will welcome us with open arms,' she replied, adding some mushrooms into the makeshift pot made out of coconut shell.

'My coming with you to Kundina is out of the question, Damayanti.'

'Why so?'

Nal looked lovingly at her. 'Your father's house is like my own, I know. But there I will not go with you in this distressed and fallen state. He saw me in all my kingly glory when I won your hand at the swayamvara and his heart had swelled with joy and pride. If I return with you thus, I will be only be shaming him with my presence. I will not be the cause of his misery and grief at seeing us reduced to such a sorry state.'

Damayanti remained adamant: 'Then I am not going alone, without you. I will not under any circumstances leave you to bear the brunt of the cruel hand that fate has dealt us. My heart at least feels lighter knowing it was not your fault at the game of dice that you lost all, but it was through sheer envy and deceit that Kali, with the help of that other demon Dwapara, maneuvered your downfall. At the same time, I will say this: Although they were the perpetrators, you were the instrument. And, the instrument was weakened by his own passion for the *chauras* and the die. Anyway that is all behind us and it is of no use being wise after the event. Today has been a particularly bad day for you, but at least now you know the truth of the matter and who was behind all this misfortune. Come, now, let us eat in peace.'

But sleep was not forthcoming and was not likely to at any time soon felt Nal, as he lay beside Damayanti staring at the night sky. He tried counting the stars but soon got muddled and gave that up. His mind went back to that day when he had felt not quite himself after the evening prayer. Then suddenly it struck him! That evening after his ablutions, he had forgotten to wash his feet and stepped into the puja room to recite the evening prayers. He had been unclean and... yesss...that is when Kali had seized the opportunity to possess him! Yes, that was it! He had felt a kind of a seizure pass through him. After that day, it had been downhill all the way and from the looks of it the speed had picked up just when he had begun to think that things couldn't get any worse. Whatever lay before him, he could not, and would not, allow Damayanti to become part of it. *No... never! She has suffered enough already!* he thought. Sitting up, he leaned forward to stoke the coals and lay back until his frazzled mind finally succumbed to sleep.

The next day, Nal told his wife that they should think of leaving the forest sanctuary. 'Why? Where will we go in our present state?' she queried.

'We cannot stay holed up here, Damayanti. I need to find some work with which we will be able to clothe and feed ourselves and that work I can only find in some nearby town. I am an expert horseman and charioteer, maybe I can put my talents to good use in some ironsmith's workshop where they make chariots, or I could work as a groom in the stables.'

'But look at me, and look at you!' she said. 'What if someone recognises us?'

'The way we look now, dressed in these tatters, I doubt if anyone out there is going to give us a second glance. Anyway, we shall leave at nightfall when the roads will be deserted and we can take shelter at some wayside inn for weary travellers.'

As night fell, and before they left, Damayanti tore off a strip from her garment and handed it to her husband. 'This will serve as a loincloth for you.' Coming to a crossroad on the highway Nal stopped to tell her, 'Look Damayanti, from here the four roads lead to the four kingdoms that lie beyond. This road takes one towards the Riskshavat mountains and the city of Avanti. That one to the left leads to Kundina, your native place in the Vidarbha region. The one to the right leads towards the great city of Ayodhya, the kingdom of the Kosalas. And going southwards, this road takes one to the lands and kingdoms lying far beyond the ones neighbouring ours.'

'But why are you telling me all this? Are you asking me which road we should take at this time of the night?'

'No, I am just saying this for your knowledge because you have never really been out of Kundina, and the only other place you have seen is Giriprastha. It is good to know something about the geography of our land. Of course, I know the road we should now take that will lead us to the nearest wayside caravan serai,' he said smiling down at her.

Arriving at the wayside inn in the dead of night they were met by a watchman who was alerted by the barking of some dogs. 'Who on earth has arrived at this hour!' he muttered to himself as he came up swinging his oil lantern. Holding it up to the two figures standing there, he was taken aback. 'Go away, go away… this is no place for vagabonds like you!'

'Please hear us out, brother,' begged Nal. 'My wife and I were attacked on the highway and robbed of our clothes and money. We just need some shelter for the night. We will go away at the first light of dawn.'

'No-no! You cannot stay here, all the rooms are occupied. There is no place here for you!'

Damayanti added her voice to Nal's plea: 'We will sleep anywhere, even in the cowshed. Have pity on us bhai, and shelter us for the night.'

The watchman brought his lantern up to Damayanti's face and moved by the hopeless and despairing look in her eyes, grunted: 'Well, okay, but just for tonight. You can sleep in the cowshed, there are bundles of hay there which you can use to sleep on. But both of you must leave by the morning.'

'Can we get something to eat, brother? My wife hasn't…'

'Are you mad? The guests ate long back and there will be nothing left in the kitchen!'

'Will you please let my wife just take a look? Maybe there are still some scraps of food lying around in the utensils! We are starving!' Nal said rubbing a hand on his bare stomach.

The watchman rubbed his chin. *The woman looks as if she will faint anytime.* Then making up his mind, he took the keys from his pocket and jangling them said, 'Come, you can see if there is anything left over in the kitchen.'

A cow mooed as Damayanti entered the barn with some food she had salvaged from the kitchen. Nal had already spread a thick, comfortable layer of straw for them and lit a lantern he had found hanging on a nail hammered into one of the poles. The warm, sweet smell of the hay permeated the barn. She sat down and they both started to eat from the only clean copper platter she had found in the kitchen.

'You must be really tired Damayanti,' Nal said. 'Lie down now and try to get some sleep. There is still plenty of time before the day breaks, and you should feel rested before we set out again. I'm just stepping out to answer a call of nature.'

'I will lie awake until you come.'

But when Nal came back, he found her asleep with an arm flung over her eyes. But sleep eluded his own eyes as he lay alongside. His mind was troubled and speculating over many 'what ifs'. By the look of things, the future appeared very bleak. He had no clue what he could or would do to improve their circumstance. It would be cruel to subject Damayanti to such an uncertain life, not knowing where and when the next meal would be coming from. It was a hopeless situation made more untenable by the malicious workings of Kali who still continued to possess his mind and body. He longed to puff at a rolled-up tobacco leaf! A thought struck him: *Maybe the watchman might have one!* The more he thought about it, greater the desire to smoke arose with him until it became unbearable. He quietly slipped out of the barn and went to see if he could find him.

'Bhaiya,' he said shaking the watchman's shoulder. 'Do you have a rolled leaf of tobacco? I am really desperate to smoke one.'

Half-opening his eyes, the watchman drew out one that was tucked behind his ear. 'Here, take this. A man needs one occasionally to relieve his tensions. Light it from the flame burning in the lantern. Smoke it outside the barn, we don't want it burning down during the night.'

Nal leaned against the door of the barn and as he inhaled, he felt a shudder ripple through his body and a deep contented sigh escaped his lips. He closed his eyes and inhaled again. *I have to decide what is best for Damayanti. She will be better off without me at this stage. But how do I convince her to go back to her father's house? She will never leave me alone in such dire straits.*

He realised he was still holding onto the burnt-out end of the rolled-up tobacco leaf. Throwing it aside he went into the barn and lay down on the mat alongside Damayanti. The intoxicant had soothed his mind, his eyelids felt heavy and sleep came quickly.

It was still pre-dawn when the raucous crowing of the cock pierced his ears. Turning over onto his side, he saw Damayanti was still fast asleep. Making sure his movements did not wake her, he quietly sat up rubbing the sleep out of his eyes. *It has to be done... and what has to be done, must be done in the instant!* 'But what will happen to her?' And his mind answered, *What will happen, will happen... she is strong-willed and she will find her way.*

But he just couldn't go out half-naked into the world outside. Looking around he saw a spear standing in a corner. He quietly picked it up and very carefully cut a piece of cloth from Damayanti's garment, which would be sufficient to cover his upper body. He then let himself quietly out of the barn, making sure he closed the door behind him. There was a faint glow in the sky. None of the inmates of the inn had yet stirred and there was a stillness hanging over the place. He hesitated and looked back at the barn behind whose door Damayanti was asleep.

Thrice he went some way. Thrice he retraced his footsteps to where she lay. *No, there is no going back... I have to leave her now because she will never leave me once she wakes up!* With that thought in mind and a heart that was heavy with sorrow, Nal finally walked out of the gates of the serai. Every step now took him further and further away from her.

Chapter 18

At The Crossroad

Damayanti was roused from sleep by a pounding on the door. Someone was shouting, 'Wake up! Wake up! It's time for you all to go!' Her eves still shut, she turned on her side to shake Nal awake, her hand felt around for his body. Alarmed, her eyes flew wide open – Nal was nowhere to be seen! *Perhaps he has just stepped out,* she thought, hastily arranging her garment as she went to open the door.

'I had told your husband and you to leave at the first light of day! Why are you still here? Do you want me to get kicked out of my job? Where is your man... find him and get going!' the watchman ordered impatiently.

'He must be outside somewhere... I will go look for him!' Damayanti quickly walked out, looked here and there but seeing no sign of Nal, she called out to him several times but got no response. With a sinking heart she retraced her steps to the barn. She splashed some water on her face from a wooden bucket that was nearby and as she lifted the hem of her garment to wipe it dry, she saw that a piece had been roughly ripped away from it.

He has deserted me!

The forewarning she had had of this when he had pointed out the roads and where they led to from the crossroad and his somewhat awkward explanation had been a ruse to quell the thought that had then risen in her mind. *'He probably hasn't gone too far... he must have gone towards the forest we left a day ago!'* Taking a few fistfuls of cattle feed and wrapping it up in a bundle of straw, Damayanti left the inn and made her way towards the only sanctuary she could think of – the forest which both of them had just recently left behind. *'Surely Nal must have retreated there to think out his next move,'* she thought. Clad in just a shred of garment, her eyes darting here and there, she kept calling out his name but her calls were met with silence. She paused to catch her breath and sat under the shade of the leafy boughs of a fragrant jasmine tree. She was half-conscious of a slithering sound that rustled through the boughs and before she knew it was trapped in the coils of a serpent that had snaked down and was now hissing at her. In her panic, she called out 'Nal! Nal! Help me!'

Hearing someone rushing through the forest towards her, her hopes lifted that Nal had finally heard her cries and was coming to her rescue. But what emerged from the thicket was a huntsman who, seeing a maiden trapped in the coils of a thick, sinuous serpent, quickly shot his arrows and freed her from its grasp. Giving her water to drink from the earthen flask strapped to his waist, he asked what a lone maiden was doing in the forest. Calmed by the presence of another human being, Damayanti narrated how she had been separated from her husband and had come searching for him in the forest. While she spoke, the strapping young huntsman could not help but cast sidelong glances every now and then at her half-clad figure in a tattered remnant of cloth. As he kept making reassuring sounds at every pause she took in the course of pouring out her troubles and woes, a hot flush of desire for the beauteous maiden before him stirred his blood and senses. Damayanti sensed that he had gradually crept closer to her under the pretext of comforting her, but now she could almost smell the heat of his body and the glimmer of lust that suddenly dilated the pupils of his eyes.

'You have had a very rough time, fair maiden. But have no fear, I am now here to protect and keep you safe. Come, let us lie together for a while before we make our way out of this forest.'

But Damayanti, sensing his real intent, shrank back and summoning her last ounce of courage shouted, 'Get away from me! How dare you even think such lustful thoughts of a noble, married woman! I am a *pativrata*, the virtuous wife of a king. I curse you to perish this very instant!' And right before her eyes, the huntsman fell dead and turned to ashes. But then the ashes rose up in a swirl of dust spiralling upwards and there emerged a cackle of wicked laughter. Kali, who in the guise of the huntsman had accosted her, now mocked Damayanti. 'I could not make you mine at your swayamvara, and I could not possess you bodily now. I have been thwarted and scorned twice. I made your lives miserable earlier when I made that fool of your husband lose everything in the game of dice. I curse you Damayanti, and your husband Nal, to a wretched life hereafter as well. May you never know an iota of happiness.'

After roaming for days, her heart lifted when she came upon some ascetics in a hermitage deep in the heart of the forest. Among the ancient rishis who graced this sacred dwelling were Bhrigu, Vashishta and Atri. Seeing a half-dazed, semi-clad woman approaching them with faltering steps, one of them came forward. Relieved to be in the presence of such holy men, Damayanti bowed and offered salutations to each of them.

'What brings you to this wilderness and why are you in such a distressed state, fair lady?' asked the ascetic. 'Come rest awhile and tell us who you are and what you seek.' Then beckoning to an acolyte, he told him to bring some food and a robe for their guest. Turning to Damayanti, he bid her to eat and asked her again, 'What are you seeking?' Addressing the sages, Damayanti recounted her tale up to the stage when Nal, in his distress, deserted her at the inn.

'What kind of man is this who would desert his wife in such extreme circumstances?' they exclaimed in unison.

'My husband Nal, once the Chakravartin king of Nishadha, deserted me because he found there was no other way to send me back to my father's house and to my children. He knew that I would never leave his side even in most trying situations and he could not see me having to bear the brunt of his wrong decisions. With Kali dogging his every move, he realised that things could get far worse than they already were. I thought he may have revisited this forest. Has he stopped by your hermitage, like I have?'

'No, we have not seen him here, fair one. He also must have thought the forest would be the first place you would search for him, so he must have avoided this place altogether. Perhaps he has gone in some other direction, or maybe he has gone back to his native place?'

'No, but where else could he have gone?' wondered Damayanti.

The hermits closed their eyes and meditated awhile. They then pronounced that a time would come when all her troubles would be over and she would be reunited with her husband and they would live a happy life together. Damayanti folded her hands and bowed her head to receive the blessing of the sages. As she raised her head she saw, much to her surprise, that they along with the hermitage had simply vanished into thin air and there was nothing there but the birds in the trees and the trees in the forest. The only proof that she had actually seen them was the physical presence of the robe she was wearing on her body. She now realised that they had appeared in a vision to bolster her courage and resolve. Thanking them with all her heart, Damayanti pushed on ahead and coming to an Ashoka tree, she rested awhile in its welcoming shade. Strangely enough, she somehow felt the sorrow lifting from her heart and putting aside the grimness of recent events dozed off to sleep.

At first she felt rather than heard the ground faintly thudding beneath her. Startled, Damayanti sat up and put her palms flat on the ground. 'Yes...' she thought. There was a rumbling sound that seemed to be drawing near. She strained her ears to hear and discerned that they were the slow, heavy footfalls of elephants combined with the faster trotting of horses that was drumming in her ears. Distant sounds of men chatting among themselves now drifted closer and she guessed that in all likelihood a caravan was passing by, which meant that she was not too far away from a main road leading somewhere or the other. Getting up and briskly brushing the leaves and dust off her, she went in the direction where the sounds were coming from. Like a forest nymph stepping out of the woods, she stood along the edge of the road and saw the approaching caravan. At its head was a richly caparisoned elephant being prodded by his mahout and behind him sat a well-dressed merchant whose golden turban was glinting in the rays of the sun. Following the elephant was a camel train carrying bolts of colourful cloth, jars of spices and chests of jewels. Riders on horses were kicking up clouds of dust as they cantered alongside. A band of youths were singing to the accompaniment of musicians in a dialect that was unfamiliar to her. Covering her nose with one hand to ward off the dust, Damayanti started waving her hand to attract the attention of a cartload of colourfully dressed women who, on spotting her, asked the boy driving the cart to pull out from the formation and stop near the woman who was waving so frantically at them.

'Ehh... yein aitu, ni yaar idhi, ill yein madakati di?' asked one of the older women in the group whose earlobes hung low with heavy gold earrings.

Damayanti looked confused as she had not understood what the woman was saying, but then she guessed from the way the woman was gesticulating that she was asking where she was from. Damayanti pointed backwards at the forest and indicated that she could not understand the language in which the woman was talking to her. She pointed at some of the members in the caravan train and repeated one word, *'Marathi, Marathi?'* pointing at her tongue. The older woman nodded and shouted out to someone in the group. A young lad came running up and said, 'Amma…hey kaye aahe? (What is it, mother?)'

'Ask this woman who she is and where she wants to go?'

Speaking to Damayanti in her language, the youth translated the old woman's question. She answered him saying she wished to join the caravan and go wherever they were going. *Hmmm…* thought the older woman scrutinising her from head to toe. Then she waved her hand at the other women to make some space and signalled to Damayanti to get on to the cart. Folding her hands in thanks to the old woman, she joined the women who were obviously talking among themselves about her presence in their midst. Some time later, they pulled out tins containing snacks and offered them to her as well.

The sun was setting behind the mountain ranges and the caravan slowed down to take a side road leading away from the main highway. It headed towards a clearing in the woods through which a stream flowed and there they untethered their camels and horses so they could drink while the menfolk went around setting up camp for the night. Sitting around the campfire at night, Suchi, the headman, addressed Damayanti: 'So, who are you and what were you doing in that fearful forest? Even though you are wearing that coarse cloth robe over that sackcloth garment, your features and bearing define you as a woman of noble birth and not some pauper.'

Having narrated her tale of trials and tribulations, Damayanti asked the headman as to where their caravan was headed and learned that the merchants were going to the kingdom of Chedi to trade their goods. 'Suvahu, the truth-loving sovereign of Chedi, is a fair and kind-hearted ruler and his Queen is reputed to be a very kind and charitable lady,' added the headman. Then addressing the women, he asked them to take good care of their guest and instructed his fellowmen to retire as they had to set out early again the next morning.

Around the middle of the night, a herd of wild elephants were following the trail to their customary watering hole when they came upon the band of sleeping men, women and young boys, along with their animals, blocking their path. Alarmed, frightened and furious, they trumpeted and hurtled towards the camp trampling men and beasts underfoot. Shrieks and cries of the people mingled with those of the animals further maddened the wild elephants and death and devastation fell upon the camp. People ran helter-skelter, desperate to get out of the way of marauding elephants and panicked horses and camels.

'Forget your merchandise! Save yourselves!' bellowed the headman. 'Leave everything! Scramble to safety!'

The elephants had gone on a rampage leaving the camp in shambles. Those who had managed to save their skins got a fire going and huddled around it lamenting the loss of friends and loved ones, while others shuffled around trying to salvage whatever was left of their merchandise and wailed that they were ruined.

'How many times we have travelled this trade route and never faced any calamity!' a woman struck her forehead and moaned.

'Hadn't we offered up prayers and offerings as always to Manibhadra, chief among the Yakshas! And also appeased Vaisravana, king of the Yakshas, before leaving? Then why did they allow disaster to strike?' cried another.

'This is all because of her!' said an old crone pointing in the direction of Damayanti who was hovering on the fringes of the crackling fire. 'We should never have taken her in our midst. Just look at her! The beautiful witch! She is the cause of all this death and destruction!'

'Yes... yes... her ill fate has followed her and befallen upon us as well. Let's stone her to death!' rose a chorus of agitated voices.

'Quiet!' thundered the headman in his commanding voice. 'She is a simple damsel in distress, and isn't it humane to offer succour to the needy? You all saw her pitiable condition and took pity on her when we took her in. She is not to blame for this.'

'Then who is to blame for this calamity?' they asked despairingly.

'No one is to blame. It was an unfortunate tragedy that a herd of wild, thirsty elephants happened to come upon us. The odour of camels, horses and tame elephants seemed to have alerted them to some kind of danger and they charged upon our camp,' reasoned the headman.

'Indeed!' said a brahmin priest who was accompanying the caravan. 'The woman is not the cause, and not to be blamed! Let us all now get some rest. The kingdom of Suvahu is not too far now and we can all do with a good night's sleep. There is a lot to do the in morning before we can break camp and leave.'

The people dispersed and as silence descended upon the camp, Damayanti quietly left the camp and went in a northerly direction where she knew the caravan would be heading much later the next day.

Chapter 19

Venom Of Karkotaka

It was still light when Nal reached the crossroad from where he had pointed out to Damayanti the directions in which the four roads branching off from it led just a day ago. He now stood there wondering which way he should go. Then thinking that with daybreak travellers would start appearing along the roads and seeing him with several days' growth of straggly hair and beard, clad in just half a tattered garment, might mistake him for a vagabond waiting to rob the unwary traveller, he stepped off the highway and walked towards the tree line beyond which lay a dense forest. Tired as he was, not having slept a wink the preceding night, he thought it best to rest awhile and get some sleep. Waking up refreshed, he would be in a better frame of mind when he could think clearly and decide on his next course of action.

He must have slept for just a couple of hours when he stirred as the smell of something burning assailed his nostrils and smoke stung his eyes. Pulling himself up to lean against the trunk of the tree, he rubbed his eyes open and to his horror saw that a part of the forest was on fire. Over the crackling flames he heard a voice screaming, 'Save me… hurry… someone please save me!'

Nal ran towards the fire and, spotting an opening, jumped

into the conflagration. A gigantic snake raised its head from its writhing coils and in a human voice pleaded piteously, 'Save me, please… get me out of here!'

'Don't panic!' cried Nal, 'I am here.' Then gauging the length and weight of the tremulous creature, Nal exclaimed, 'But how will I lift you… you are far too huge and heavy!'

'I am the naga Karatoka, a semi-divine snake with magical powers. Wait… I will shrink myself to fit into the palm of your hand! Just reach out your hand and touch me on the head.' And at his touch, much to the astonishment of Nal, the snake instantly shrank before his eyes. He then reached out and picked up Karkotaka from the circle of fire and took him to safety. Finding a cool rock, as Nal made to put him down, Karkotaka said, 'Wait, King Nal… don't put me down here!'

'How do you know who I am?' Nal froze in his tracks, taken aback.

Karkotaka raised his now tiny-as-a-pinhead to look at him. 'Rishi Narad had predicted that one day you would come and only you would save me! I have waited hundreds of years for this moment. Now please do as I tell you. Take ten steps in that direction slowly while I tell you my story and keep counting the steps as you take them.'

'What a strange creature you are!' said Nal. 'Anyway, I will do as you say.'

'You won't regret it! Okay, so I had in some way offended Rishi Narad, the messenger of the gods, and he placed a curse on me that I would become immobile as a stone unless and until Nal, the virtuous one, came along and freed me from his curse.'

'Can't you see how my so-called virtue rewarded, or should I say punished, me? From a Chakravartin monarch, I have been reduced to a half-naked pauper, banished from my kingdom, bereft of my lovely wife whom I have forsaken and left to her fate.'

'All that was due to a simple oversight when unclean, you entered the prayer room and offered prayers. Kali seized that moment to enter you and possess your mind and body, and dispossess you of your kingship, honour, and even your high-born, beautiful wife. Be grateful he could not touch your soul.'

'There is little to be grateful for, when everything else has been lost,' answered a mournful Nal.

'Stop right there!' commanded Karkotaka. 'That was your ninth step! Now after taking your tenth step, pause and then put me down on that rock there.'

As Nal bent to put him down, Karkotaka bit him on the wrist and his venom surged into Nal's bloodstream.

Nal screamed in agony. 'Is this how you repay me for my goodness!'

'I've only done that which is in a snake's nature to do… and that is to bite! However, don't worry… you won't die from it. But in a matter of seconds now, you will no longer remain the same.'

And as the poison spread into his system, Nal felt his form shrinking till he resembled a misshapen human being. Simultaneously, from a tiny snake, Karkotaka moved his sleek coils and assumed his gigantic form once again.

Horrified, Nal stared at his hands and feet. His hands flew to his face and felt the boils that had sprouted on his forehead and cheeks. 'What is this!' he screamed in fright. 'What have you done to me!'

'Fear not, Nal. Look at it as a blessing in disguise,' comforted Karkotaka. 'With the powers I now have at my command, I have altered your shape and features into this form so that no one can recognise you as the former Chakravartin monarch of Nishadha. While my venom will not cause you any physical discomfort or pain, it will torment and cause immense anguish to Kali, the demon who still possesses your mind and dwells in your body. My poison will invade his spirit and in insufferable agony will he remain imprisoned within you until he can bear it no longer. He will ultimately be compelled to leave your body and thus you will be delivered from his evil possession. Look upon it not as my ingratitude, but as my blessing and thanks to you for having relieved me from the curse of Narad.'

'But now misshapen with a hunchback and looking so hideous, where can I go? People will turn away after looking at me! Who will hire me or give me shelter?' Nal said in desperation.

'I have just told you that this transformation I have imposed on you will be both a disguise and a blessing in the days to come,' placated Karkotaka. 'Hear me out. Your instinctive understanding of horses and bonding with them is what makes you one of the most skilled charioteers in the land of Bharatvarsha. I know for a fact that king Rituparna, scion of the Ikshvaku dynasty, is in dire need of a personal charioteer. Go north to Ayodhya and present yourself to the monarch as Vahuka, the charioteer. Rituparna is a kind man and places great value on talent and skills. Why, he himself is a skilled player of dice. You are pretty good at it too but there is none better than him in the entire land. If he develops a liking to you, which he will, maybe you can learn how to play it as well as him, if not better.'

Nal ran his fingers through his hair, nonplussed by what Karkotaka had just said. 'Will I ever get to see the wife I deserted and my children again? Even if I were to see them, will they ever recognise or even accept me in this horribly misshapen form?'

'Do not look so dejected and become sorrowful, Nal,' said Karkotaka, and using his special powers manifested two shimmering garments that were made of some cloth the likes of which Nal had never seen before. 'Here are garments made of celestial cloth. Keep them safe and do not appear wearing them before Rituparna. Whenever the time should come that you will wish to regain your former royal bearing and form, put these on and you will be made whole.'

As Nal took both the garments in his hands and was admiring their workmanship, he head Karkotaka say, 'It is time for me to take my leave of you.'

'Farewell Karkotaka,' Nal said.

'Farewell Nal, and my blessings be upon you.'

Wrapping the fine garments in a bundle of plantain leaves, Nal headed north toward Ayodhya.

Chapter 20

Maid In Waiting

'Pagli, pagli...'

'Chudail...'

'Hatt... duur hatt!'

As Damayanti entered the city gates of Suktimati-Puri, capital of the Chedi kingdom, her bedraggled hair, her eyes darting nervously here and there, her unkempt appearance attracted stares from people in the marketplace. A band of rowdy, jeering children dogged her footsteps, with some of them even making bold to hurl pebbles and stones at her retreating form. As she neared the main square which was overlooked by the balustrades of the city palace, a sizeable crowd had gathered and the jeering and heckling had become so loud that it attracted the attention of Sagarika, the wife of King Suvahu, who was sitting on her balcony overlooking the city square.

'Why on earth is the crowd harassing that poor creature down there!' Sagarika asked the nurse who always attended on her. 'Go down and drive those leering men and the children who are troubling her away, and bring that unfortunate woman here to me.'

The attendant rushed down and waved her hands to push back the crowd. 'Get away, get away from her you idiots!' she shouted. Then addressing Damayanti, she said, 'Come with me!

The Queen Mother has summoned you into her presence.' Then as she guided her through the palace, he added: 'Remember to keep your eyes lowered and bow as you approach her.'

'Come, come closer…' The Queen Mother, Sagarika, said in her gentle, coaxing tone as she looked up and down at Damayanti who, even in her sorry state, still possessed a certain dignity and radiated a luminosity that made Sagarika remark, 'Although you appear fallen on hard times, you do not appear to be some lowly creature. Your unearthly beauty shines like lightning through dark clouds. Who are you my child and how come you are in the land of Chedi?'

Bowing with folded hands, Damayanti replied, 'Gentle mother, I am a woman deserted. My husband, who lost everything in a game of dice could no longer support me or bear to see me brought so low through his misfortune. I would have never left his side even in his bad times, but he left me in the middle of the night and disappeared. I know not where he is and in what state. Not knowing where to go, I joined a caravan of merchants who was coming to your kingdom and have arrived here this very day.'

Turning to her nurse attendant, Sagarika instructed her to get something to eat and drink for the visitor. Then patting Damayanti on her shoulder, she said: 'You are welcome to stay here. I will help you in any way I can to find your husband. I will send some of our trusted men to search for him. And, who knows, he, feeling repentant at having left you alone to fend for yourself, just might accidentally turn up here just like you have today. The love you bear for each other will one day surely reunite you. One should not lose hope.'

Hearing these heartwarming words, Damayanti's eyes welled with tears. Brushing them away with the back of her hand, she said, 'You are indeed very kind, Queen Mother. I will be happy if you take me as your serving lady. But, I have a few reservations about staying in this huge palace and would like to state them, if you will give your permission for me to speak plainly and without fear.'

'Of course, my child… what is it you wish to say?'

Now, for the first time, Damayanti raised her head to look the Queen Mother in the eyes. 'Kind mother, I, being a married lady will not eat the leavings of any other besides my husband. I will not wash or touch anyone else's feet. Let no man here covet me or desire to marry me. If any man here attempts to do so, I would request you to have him punished. Should you send your trusted men to search for my husband, I would like to talk to them before they leave. Can I be assured of all his?'

'Yes, I give you my solemn word it shall be as you desire,' assured Sagarika.

'Then I will gladly accept to be with you as your serving maid,' assented Damayanti.

'A serving maid! Not at all my dear!' exclaimed Sagarika. She told her nurse attendant to fetch her daughter Sunanda. 'Tell her to come immediately.'

'Yes mother, you sent for me?' Sunanda asked as she walked in briskly.

'Yes, Sunanda… I want you to meet this young lady here who I have hired to be your companion… your *sairandhri.* Take her with you to your chambers and be good to her…'

'As you wish, mother...' A cheerful girl, Sunanda smiled at Damayanti and exclaimed, 'You are so beautiful! Come, we must get you into some decent clothes first…' Taking her hand, she led her out of the Queen Mother's chamber, then pausing asked, 'But what is your name? Mother did not mention that…'

'Princess, if you like you can call me Sairandhri,' smiled Damayanti.

Long after it had happened, the news that Nal had deserted Damayanti at a wayside inn reached King Bhima by a circuitous route. The caravan that had dropped her off at Suktimati-Puri wound its way to Kundina one fine day and set up camp on the outskirts of the capital city. During the day, the men and womenfolk would come to the main square and set up makeshift stalls displaying their wares. A visiting caravan always evoked great excitement among the citizens and they would flock to see the latest collection of dazzling bolts of cloth, gemstones and jewellery, inlaid swords and daggers and other such decorative items. Amid the hubbub and hustle-bustle, news and gossip from afar and near flew fast and thick among the crowd.

At one such gaily decorated stall, some women from the palace, while striking bargains, were being entertained by a spicy piece of gossip being bandied about by the talkative gypsy woman who had set up her stall at a vantage place. The women were all ears as she told them about a wild-looking woman with unwashed, matted hair who had stepped out of the forest half-naked wearing a tattered garment. 'Believe me, at first I thought it was some *yakshini* of the forest – yes… yes… her beauty shone through all the grime and dust on her face and body! She was a sight to see… even the horses and camels nervously neighed and grunted as she came nearer! She babbled something about being a Queen! Can you imagine that!' she added for good measure. She went on to add that the poor creature looked as if she hadn't eaten for days! Taking pity on her, the gypsy woman had given her something to eat and drink and the headman of the caravan had, out of the goodness of his heart, allowed her to join the caravan which was then on its way to the kingdom of Chedi.

Among the group of women listening to this bit of spicy news was the chief handmaiden to the Queen Mother. While massaging the Queen's feet at night she narrated the gossip she had heard from the gypsy woman. 'Who could she possibly be?' wondered the handmaiden.

Far away in Kundina, Damayanti's mother Charumati's mind was troubled. When King Bhima came to her bedchamber that night, she told him, 'We haven't had any word from Damayanti after she sent the children to us. How she is, where both she and Nal are now, we have had no news of them for so long! Today, my maid brought a strange bit of news about an incident which I gather happened some time ago on the crossroad from where the roads branch out in four directions. Perhaps it is in some way connected with our beloved daughter Damayanti, who could be traced in Chedi. In fact, that is where my sister Sagarika, the queen of King Suvahu resides!'

'Why do you want to follow up on some wild tale passed on by a passing caravan of trade merchants?' queried Bhima. 'Our Nal, although fallen on bad days, is a good man and Damayanti worships the ground he walks on. She must be by his side, wherever they may be.'

'No Bhima, I have an uneasy feeling about this… something is wrong, somewhere. Else wouldn't we have had some word from them by now? There has been none!' insisted Charumati.

'Do you seriously believe this to be connected somehow to our Damayanti? This is really absurd!' remarked the king. 'Anyway, just so that you don't worry your pretty little head too much about it, I will send some trustworthy men to Chedi and the nearabout towns and cities to make some discreet enquiries.'

'Thank you Bhima,' she said, handing him a goblet of wine. 'I think that is very wise of you, my dear husband. Now tell me… how are our sons shaping up in the military academy?'

Chapter 21

The Stables Of Ayodhya

'A city built by God' is how the Atharvaveda described Ayodhya, which lay on the right bank of the River Saryu. It was the capital of the ancient kingdom of Kosala and was said to have been founded by King Ayudh from whom the city got its name. Under the reign of King Rituparna, the son of King Ayutaswa, the city had prospered and was renowned as being among the nine sacred cities of Bharatvarsha.

On the tenth day after having been transformed by the bite of Karkotaka, Nal entered the gates of Ayodhya. As he was walking past the stables, he saw a magnificent steed fidgeting and stomping its hooves while being rubbed down the wrong way by a groom who did not seem to know the proper way of doing even this simple task. Unable to see the discomfort of the horse, Nal walked up and told the groom to step aside for a while. To his surprise, he saw Nal go up to the horse and while stroking its neck whisper something into the animal's ear. This seemed to calm it down and it now stood quietly while Nal began brushing its coat.

'Can you talk to horses? That one there is a hot-headed one! What did you whisper into his ear that made him quiet as a lamb?' asked the amazed groom. 'I have not seen you around here before... where do you come from and what is your name?'

Nal turned to smile at the youth while carrying on brushing its coat, 'I am called Vahuka, and I have a natural gift for communicating with horses and getting them to do my bidding. I have come here looking for employment.'

'My name is Jivala,' said the youth. 'Wait till I tell the Master of the Horse about your talents, he will surely wish to use your services!'

And so it was that Nal began working in the stables of Ayodhya. As stories began to circulate about his way with horses, word of it soon also reached the ears of Rituparna whose chief attendant one day summoned Nal to present himself before the king. Making himself as presentable as he could, Nal appeared and bowed low to the king.

'I have been hearing about the amazing way you have with horses, and the other morning one of my men espied you tethering four of them to a chariot and exercising them in the grounds behind the palace. From where have you acquired such skills?'

'It's a natural gift Your Majesty… as for my skills as a charioteer, I had been taught by the best as a young man,' said Nal, keeping his eyes lowered while addressing Rituparna.

'How would you like to become my personal charioteer? You shall be well paid for looking after the horses and also training them to drive the chariot – in precision as if they were not four but one, each instinctively matching stride with the others so that I become the fastest charioteer in the land,' asked the king.

'You do me a great honour, O King!' Nal said with gratitude. 'I shall strive to do my best.'

'Good,' said the monarch. 'I will depute Varshaneya and Jivala to be your assistants, so they may also get trained under your guidance.'

In time, Rituparna came to rely on Nal and as they would ride in the chariot something similar to a mutual regard developed between the two men. One evening when the King along with some of his friends were at their evening meal, the guests were going into raptures over the culinary skills of the king's kitchen. Rituparna also realised that the food that was being served this evening was truly exceptional – the likes of which had never before emerged from the royal kitchens. After the guests had departed, he called for the chief steward and asked him if he had hired new cooks. When the steward replied in the negative, the King asked, 'Then how come this evening's meal tasted so very different and more delicious than the usual food that comes out of the kitchens?'

'One of the cooks was absent today Your Majesty, so Vahuka offered to help out in the kitchen today in cutting the vegetables and marinating the meat. When he saw the cooks going about it in the usual way, he laughed and said, 'Is this the way you prepare the food for our King? Move aside, let me show you how to prepare food that leaves the guests licking their fingers and asking for more!' Saying which, he garnered all the condiments and spices and deftly went about mixing them in his own way. He almost took over the kitchen saying that the rest of the staff could watch while he prepared this evening's meal.'

'Hmmm…' Rituparna tapped his chin thoughtfully. *Who is this strange creature Vahuka? An ace charioteer and an epicurean as well? Perhaps I should get to know him better!*

One day as they were racing their chariots, Rituparna, coming close on the wheels of Vahuka's chariot reined in his horses and said, 'Will I ever be as good a charioteer as you, Vahuka?'

Such an opportunity was one that Nal had been waiting for all this time. He turned to Rituparna and said, 'You are already very good my King, but I could help you become a champion. But for that, you will need to spare some time so I can pass on my art and skill in handling the horses and the chariot expertly.'

'Done!' said Rituparna vigorously. 'For that I will double your pay for that and also give you a parcel of land.'

'My pay is already very generous, my King, but…' said Nal and hesitated.

'But what, Vahuka? What else could you possibly want?

Out with it!'

'I dare not ask...' Nal still hesitated.

'What is it that you want, Vahuka! Don't be afraid... say it... you have my word, if it is in my power to give, I shall give it gladly.'

'Then in return I ask that you teach me your knowledge of mathematics and the skills that you employ in winning every game of dice. I have heard there is none better than you in all the land,' Nal blurted in one fast breath, before he lost his nerve.

Rituparna laughed. 'And why do you want to acquire mastery over the dice, Vahuka? It is a game of precision and skill I agree, but it is also a game of chance. What do you hope to win?'

Nal smiled weakly. 'The sheer pleasure one derives from winning, my King.'

'Fine!' Rituparna thumped him on the back. 'We shall meet for a game every evening and I shall teach you all the techniques, calculations and above all – the tricks of the game that can be employed to defeat the opponent.'

By now Nal, as Vahuka, had formed quite a good rapport with his assistants Varshaneya and Jivala and the three of them had almost taken over the day-to-day management of the royal stables. In the evening when the day was done, Nal would come to his quarters and sit there brooding, his thoughts invariably returning to the night when he had left Damayanti while she was asleep at the wayside inn. He would often lament to himself, *I wonder where she will be, helpless, hungry and weary of facing the hardships of life without a husband to provide for her. Where would she have gone? Where could she be now?*

Varshaneya had, unknown to Nal, often heard him cry his heart out and one evening made bold to ask what troubled him and why he appeared so mournful and distressed every night. Unable to suppress his anguish any longer, Nal unburdened his heart and without mentioning his own and Damayanti's name, he narrated the full trials and tribulations that he had undergone since the disastrous game of dice.

Varshaneya was sympathetic and asked, ‘Vahuka, now where is this friend of yours who deserted his wife and left her alone to grapple with the hardships of a lone, married woman in this harsh world?’

‘Who knows where that wretched man must be? But wherever he is, I am certain he is being punished and suffering for the dastardly deed of deserting his wife.’

‘But he must have presumed that his wife would eventually find her way back to her father’s house and that she would be safe and looked after there. She is probably at her father’s house now. So, don’t judge your friend too badly Vahuka. He had his own compulsions and let us admit, he acted in the best interests of his wife,’ consoled Varshaneya. ‘Anyway don’t distress yourself unnecessarily, I am sure they must both have found safe sanctuary.’

And so the days went by, being spent in teaching King Rituparna the art of becoming a skilled horseman and an ace charioteer. The evenings were devoted to the game of dice and in teaching Vahuka to master the game.

‘I still don’t know what you are going to gain from mastering the dice, Vahuka,’ the king would often remark. ‘But, I may say you are getting better at it day by day. Why, I could wager that you almost play it as if your life depended on it!’ joked Rituparna.

Part 3

A Search For The Lovers

Chapter 22

NEEDLES IN A HAYSTACK

North, South, East and West they went. Dressed as craftsmen, traders and even brahmin priests, the emissaries of King Bhima went out in pairs scouring the cites, towns and villages. But they did not find anyone who had seen a man resembling Nal or a woman like Damayanti. How could they when the descriptions they were giving were of the royal couple they had once known? It was like looking for needles in a haystack! They had no way of knowing that Nal had been transformed into a misshapen, unrecognisable man with a hunchback, and that Damayanti was living out her life masquerading as a serving woman in some far-off city.

Months went by but so far there was no one who had heard of anyone remotely resembling either Nal or Damayanti. Back in Kundina, King Bhima and his Queen had almost given up hope when Dana, one of Damayanti's brothers, brought word that a person, who had accompanied his good friend Sudeva, had just returned and sought an audience with the King. Apparently Sudeva in his search had, after many days, arrived at the kingdom of Chedi and had sent a piece of news through this messenger.

'But why hasn't Sudeva come himself, Dana?' asked Charumati.

'He is still in Chedi your Highness, trying to ferret out some more information that may help him locate the whereabouts of the woman he thinks could possibly be princess Damayanti.' replied the messenger.

'Sudeva is a bright young man, my dear,' Bhima said turning to his wife. 'We can hope to hear some good news from him in the next few weeks. We must wait patiently.'

'Bhima, you know that my sister is married to King Suvahu of Chedi. Let me send word to her through this courier, to see if she can possibly be of any help!'

'No my dear, let us not do that just yet. Let us not air our family troubles abroad. We must wait for some firm news from Sudeva before taking any such action,' said Bhima firmly.

'But I am so worried about Damayanti! God alone knows in what condition she may be!' cried his wife.

'Wherever she is, she will certainly be with Nal... so let us not despair!' comforted Bhima.

Dismissing the messenger, the King told him to rest a day or two before rejoining Sudeva.

Meanwhile, Sudeva who one afternoon was watching some children playing outside the palace walls of Suktimati, saw two women step out from the rear gates of the palace. The younger of the two was obviously a lady of regal bearing while the older one, although dressed in simpler attire, had an air of authority about her. As they passed by, Sudeva observed that there was something about her, he couldn't put his finger on it, that reminded him of the princess Damayanti. But wait, he told himself, did not the princess Damayanti have a distinct and distinguishing mole between her eyebrows? There was no such mole that he could observe, at least not even from a close distance, on the forehead of this lady. He also noticed that while the woman had shot him a quick glance as she went by and almost frozen in mid-step, there had flashed a quick spark of recognition in her eyes which she had just as instantly dimmed. Both the ladies had, out of respect, simply nodded their heads at the brahmin, and gone on their way.

Sudeva's heart had almost leapt into his mouth at this fleeting exchange. He felt weak in the knees and sat down on a mound of bricks to collect his thoughts. Foremost among these was a question that if indeed this was Damayanti, then logically Nal should also be around here somewhere. There was only one way to resolve his doubts and that was to somehow gain entry into the palace and make further enquiries about the woman he had just seen. An opportunity soon presented itself in the form of a free lunch for brahmin priests organised by the Queen Mother in commemoration of a forthcoming festival.

Upon entering the palace on the auspicious day, Sudeva deliberately chose to sit at the very end of the row of brahmins waiting to be served the ritual meal. He was pleased to note that while the princess Sunanda was going down the line greeting each brahmin with folded hands, the woman he had seen in the market square and imagined to be Damayanti, was following behind along with other maidservants and was supervising the food being ladled onto plantain leaves placed before each brahmin. As Damayanti paused before Sudeva, the veil covering her head slid and despite her best efforts to conceal the mole under a layer of sandalwood paste, it stood revealed to him. There could be no mistaking it. Sairandhri, as Sunanda had called her name, was Damayanti! But, now what would be the best way to reveal her true identity to the Queen Mother?

After the meal, the priests stood to give their blessings to the Queen Mother as each one received a gift of a white dhoti from her. When Sudeva went up, he requested for a personal audience with the Queen Mother saying that he had something of import to tell her. In the private chamber, he introduced himself as an emissary from the court of King Bhima of Vidarbha on a mission to locate and bring back his daughter Damayanti and his son-in-law Nal of Nishadha. After months of roaming, he had visited the kingdom of Chedi and had seen a lady in the company of princess Sunanda whom he thought was princess Damayanti in disguise.

'What?' exclaimed Sagarika[1], 'My sister's daughter is living disguised as a serving maid in my own house! True, I haven't seen her since my sister gave birth to her at our father, King Sudaman's house. And I do seem to recall that the newborn had a tiny mole between her brows. But I find it hard to believe that she could be my niece. It all sounds quite preposterous!'

'Believe me, Your Highness… if you can kindly ask your daughter and her sairandhri to come here, we can soon get to hear the truth of the matter.'

When Sunanda appeared with her sairandhri in tow, they were both surprised to see the brahmin Sudeva there. Damayanti froze in her tracks! The Queen Mother beckoned her to come closer and lifted her head-covering to get a closer look at her face. She now saw a certain resemblance to her sister in the face before her.

'Sunanda,' Charumati said. 'Dip a cloth in that rosewater bowl and bring it to me.' She then proceeded to wipe off the sandalwood paste on Damayanti's brow and the mole there stood revealed! 'Yes, it is she! Damayanti, my dear child,' asked Sunanda's mother, 'why have you been hiding your true self from us for all these days?'

Damayanti broke down and tearfully narrated the course of events that had befallen them once Nal had lost his kingdom in the game of dice. At this juncture, Sudeva asked about the whereabouts of King Nal to which Damayanti replied that she had no idea whatsoever where he might be. Sunanda stepped forward and hugged Damayanti to her bosom, 'I am sorry, dear sister, if at any time I have been unkind to you.'

Clasping Sunanda to her bosom, Damayanti hushed her

1 Damayanti's aunt Sagarika, was married to Suvahu, the king of Chedi. So when she comes to know who sairandhri is, she sends her to Kundina to her mother's place.

saying, 'You have always treated me well, my dear sister.'

'Well now,' said the Queen Mother taking command of the situation. 'What do you wish to do now Damayanti?'

'Dear Aunt, I would like nothing better than to be reunited at the earliest with my children who are living with my parents in Kundina. Sudeva, whom I had recognised as my brother's dearest friend when I saw him in the marketplace, can accompany me on my return.'

Overjoyed at the turn of events, Sunanda begged her mother to allow her to accompany Damayanti to Kundina with the plea that she would love to meet young Indrasen and Indraseni, as well as her aunt and uncle.

'You shall leave on the morrow, in full regal splendour befitting your status. I shall ask your father to depute a regiment of our personal bodyguards who shall escort you and Damayanti safely to Kundina. Meanwhile, we shall also mount a discreet mission to locate her husband, Nal.'

Sudeva had thoughtfully despatched a forerunner to announce the news of Damayanti's arrival at Kundina in a few days. King Bhima and his Queen were overjoyed and the city wore a festive look with floral decorations at every pillar and post to welcome the princess home. The crowds cheered lustily when the royal train entered the city gates and followed it all the way to the palace. Waiting to receive and welcome their daughter home were King Bhima, Charumati, and Damayanti's twins Indrasen and Indraseni.

Although rejoicing at the return of their daughter Damayanti, her parents were dismayed to learn about the hardships she had to endure after Nal and she were both banished from Giriprastha. They were, moreover, left aghast on hearing about Nal's desertion but understood that he had done it as a last resort to leave Damayanti with no choice but to return to her parents and to her children.

'The children need their father, and I need my husband,' Damayanti told her parents.

'Do not despair,' said King Bhima. 'Since Sudeva has proved to be so resourceful in tracking you down to Chedi, I am certain he will be the right person to head the search for Nal.'

'But he must be made aware of some facts he so far knows nothing about,' replied Damayanti. 'I would like to share some information with him and instruct his team before they set out to find Nal.'

When Sudeva came to meet Damayanti, she said: 'You are like a brother to me now, Sudeva. When you and your men go out in all the realms in search of Nal, let two or three of them pose as balladeers and visit the marketplace where people gather and narrate this tale of love and longing: 'There once was a king who gambled and lost all he possessed and was banished into exile. Unable to bear the shame and ignominy of his deed, he even abandoned his wife. One night while she slept, he tore away half her garment to cover his body and slipped away into the darkness. She still weeps and waits for the day he will return.' However, they should on no account let my name escape their lips, nor reveal that the message comes from me.'

'It shall be as you command, Princess,' assured Sudeva. 'Since you regard me as your brother, my men and I will leave no stone unturned in our search for your husband.'

'My heart says he is out there somewhere,' said a wistful Damayanti.

Chapter 23

In Search Of Nal

The seasons came and went. Months rolled by with no word coming in from either Sudeva or any member of his team. Every night when Damayanti told bedtime stories to put her children to sleep, they never failed to ask, 'Mother, when will our father come back?' It tore at her heart when she could not give them an appropriate answer and only lull and comfort them with the words, 'Soon... very soon.'

Hope springs eternal in the human breast and so it was that one day a brahmin by the name of Parnada, a member of the team assembled by Sudeva, returned to Kundina with news that gladdened the hearts of Damayanti and her parents.

'Salutations to the Princess,' Parnada said bowing his head.

'Greetings, Parnada,' answered Damayanti coming forward. 'I hope you bear some good news which my ears have been eager to here. So far, the other messengers have had nothing to report.'

'I believe with all my heart that the news I bring will be of some import, Princess,' said Parnada. 'On the instructions of Sudeva, I followed the road that led north towards Ayodhya, the capital of the kingdom of Kosala. Luckily, we were able to join a convoy of militia that was heading there and reached Ayodhya much earlier that we had hoped. Along with my companion, who is skilled at the tanpura, we scouted the city and arriving at the market square he began to strum his tanpura to attract the crowd. I lent my voice to sing the ballad of the noble woman who had been deserted by her husband.'

'Then what happened?' Damayanti asked with bated breath.

'On listening to my song, many of the women were moved to tears, while the men whispered among themselves trying to guess who the song was about. As the crowd dispersed, I noticed a rather well-dressed, misshapen dwarf-like man who had kept himself some distance away from the crowd and now leaning against against a tree with a grieved look on his face.'

'How very strange!' remarked Damayanti. 'But surely, he could not …'

'Wait, hear me out, Princess…' pleaded Parnada. 'Later that night, a guard from the palace came searching for us at the serai we were staying at and asked us to accompany him. We were led into a well-appointed chamber and told to wait.'

'Who was it that summoned you?' asked Damayanti.

'Imagine our surprise when he turned out to be the dwarf-like man who had been grief-stricken on hearing our ballad!' exclaimed Parnada. 'He invited us to sit down and sent his attendant to get some refreshments for us. Then turning to me, he introduced himself as Vahuka, the personal charioteer of King Rituparna, and said he had been very touched by the ballad of the noble lady in distress…'

'But surely he couldn't have summoned you just to tell you that?' asked a perplexed Damayanti.

'All he said was this: *Even in extreme misery, noble women still preserve mastery over themselves… she by such a husband forsaken will not complain nor yield to anger.*' And then he said something very strange: *'He that deserted her was overwhelmed by calamities…deprived by birds of his sole garment while trying to trap them for food and sustenance.* I still can't figure out what he meant by all that!' Parnada looked at her with a puzzled expression.

The effect of his words on Damayanti was startling! Her face went white as a sheet and her voice quavered as she nervously thanked Parnada for his news. 'You have done well, Parnada… and you shall be rewarded handsomely for your news. Now, go home… you have been away from your wife and children too long and they have waiting anxiously for your return.'

As soon as he left, Damayanti rushed to her mother's chamber and threw herself in her arms. Taking her hand she placed it on her bosom, 'My heart is fluttering like a caged bird, Mother… the man that Parnada described can in no way be Nal, but the words he uttered no other man could possibly have known…'

'Calm yourself Damayanti, let us think this through,' said her mother. 'Of course, the dwarf-like charioteer cannot be Nal! Maybe Nal met him sometime during this period and unburdened his heart to him… maybe he knows something about him, or when and where he met him last!'

Damayanti drummed her temples with trembling fingers. 'My mind is racing… I cannot seem to think straight… stranger things have happened to us after we were banished from Giriprastha… we have been ruined and mocked by demons… I being blessed by illusory hermits and then being mysteriously guided to Chedi…'

'We must proceed with caution… what we do now could affect the way events unfold in the coming days,' cautioned her mother. 'Let us await Sudeva's return and consult him also on this matter.'

Sudeva returned a week later from the kingdom of Panchala and was pleased to learn the outcome of Parnada's visit to Ayodhya. However, wishing to personally hear Parnada's account, he sent for the brahmin and arranged a meeting with Damayanti and her mother also in attendance. Questioning him at various points of his narration, Sudeva also spread his hands stating, 'There is nothing definite we can deduce from this account. Yet, it is a ray of light in what earlier appeared a dark end of the tunnel. But it strikes me as very odd that a misshapen, dwarf-like figure has won the complete trust of King Rituparna inasmuch that he has become his personal counsellor, charioteer and frequent companion. Why would Rituparna entertain the proximity of such a person? There is certainly something mysterious behind all this.'

Damayanti intervened now to say, 'I have a strong feeling that the answer to all this lies in Ayodhya itself. My heart had leapt at the news Parnada had brought and I agree that there is much more to the story of this dwarf-charioteer of King Rituparna than meets the eye.'

'Whatever do you mean Damayanti?' queried her mother.

'There is one way to get Nal, wherever he is now, to return to Kundina and resolve this mystery,' Damayanti said addressing both her mother and Sudeva. 'Let us send Sudeva to Ayodhya! But meanwhile, mother, please don't say anything of this to my father!'

'But what can I accomplish by going there, Princess?'

'Sudeva, you employed amazing skills in finding me at Chedi and bringing me back to Kundina. Now, I am beseeching you to use those very skills to get to Nal, wherever he may be now. Although by Parnada's account, I am certain he has to be somewhere in or around Ayodhya.'

'And once there, how do you expect me to proceed, Princess?' Sudeva asked. 'Do you have a plan that will draw Nal out from hiding?'

Damayanti smiled. 'Yes, indeed I do, Sudeva. If my plan doesn't work, then nothing else will! Now listen carefully to what you must do, using all your tact and diplomacy, once you reach there.'

Chapter 24

Damayanti Invites Rituparna

Descended from a long line of Suryavanshi rulers, Rituparna had proved himself to be a worthy successor to his father, King Sarvakama. As a flourish of trumpets sounded, the king entered the audience chamber with a short, dwarf-like figure following close behind. There was a rustle of robes as the assembled courtiers arose to their feet as a gesture of respect to their king. Today, he was greeting emissaries from some of the neighbouring kingdoms to discuss certain territorial issues. Among the last of the emissaries to be called and presented before him was Sudeva of Vidarbha.

'So, how fares King Bhima of Vidarbha and what are the tidings your bear from him, prince Sudeva?' asked Rituparna as a matter of courtesy.

Sudeva came forward and bowed before Rituparna. 'As a matter of fact, my Lord, I bear greetings from his lovely daughter, Princess Damayanti.'

Taken by surprise, Rituparna pondered over Sudeva's statement as his mind flashed back to her swayamvara he had attended some years ago. Looking thoughtful, he asked, 'And what is it that Princess Damayanti would seek from Ayodhya? Is she visiting her parents at Kundina?'

'My Lord, she has been living with her parents for quite some time now since the disappearance of her husband, King Nal. After waiting these many years, not knowing whether King Nal lives or not, she has decided to once again hold her swayamvara and invites you to attend it,' Sudeva said respectfully, handing him a scroll. 'I have been journeying to extend the invitation to the rulers of kingdoms far and near,' he added as he had been instructed to do by Damayanti.

While he had been delivering this message, Sudeva had, with his wits about him, not failed to observe that the dwarf-like person standing behind the king's throne had visibly stiffened and appeared shaken.

'But this scroll says the swayamvara is to be held two days from now!' exclaimed an astonished Rituparna. 'How can one possibly reach there in time!' Then turning to the dwarf behind him, he asked, 'Vahuka, is it at all possible to make it to Kundina in such little time? I am determined to go!'

'May I take your leave now, Your Highness?' Sudeva asked.

'Yes-yes... indeed, and thank you for conveying the Princess's wishes,' Rituparna added.

After Sudeva had left and the business of the court had been done for the day, Rituparna sent for Vahuka. When he arrived, the King asked him: 'Now, tell me Vahuka... you are the best among charioteers, is it somehow possible to reach Kundina to attend Damayanti's swayamvara in the short time we have at our disposal?'

Vahuka hedged. He cleared his throat, 'Your Majesty, may I be permitted to say a few words of caution? You do know that the Princess Damayanti is the mother of twins?'

'Yes, I know, and it doesn't matter to me,' said Rituparna. 'She is the most beautiful and desirable woman in the land and I would be proud to win her hand in marriage.'

Vahuka bowed his head in acceptance of Rituparna's wishes. 'Then yes, my Lord, I can assure that I can drive you there well in time to attend her swayamvara.'

'Excellent!' exclaimed the King. 'Choose the steeds that are fleet-of-foot and harness them to my royal chariot. We shall leave as soon as you are ready!'

'Oh-hh… the perfidy of women!' Nal cried, banging his head against a wall, once he was alone in his quarters.

'How could you do this, Damayanti?' he wailed. 'How could you who loved me to distraction… the mother of my children, even think of marrying again? Or, is it that you are now taking revenge on my having left you sleeping and for having deserted you at that wayside inn? Is your heart so hardened against me that you have now determined to take another husband?'

A hundred doubts plagued his mind as he paced up and down rueing his fate. *Should I feign a sudden illness and let the King take another charioteer, since he is so determined to go to the swayamvara? That way he will never make the journey in time!* he thought perversely. But then another thought followed that quickly. *But what purpose will that serve? Has Damayanti deliberately arranged her second swayamvara in the hope that I will come to her any which way that I can find? She surely is aware that only I can cover the distance to Kundina in the time remaining! No-no... she has given up on me, perhaps she even thinks I am dead and gone from this earth? Or, is she now avenging my desertion of her?* Then he made up his mind. *I shall go, there is no other course left for me to follow. I cannot let Rituparna down after all he has done for me... and, what's more, I will be able to discover Damayanti's true purpose in arranging this swayamvara.*

He heard footsteps approaching and took hold of himself. The door opened and Varshaneya entered. 'The King has sent me to ask when he can come to inspect the horses, Vahuka!'

'Go, tell him they are ready. He can come now if he so wishes.'

Composing himself and steeling his nerves, Nal walked over to the King's private stables. When Rituparna arrived he was shocked to see the horses selected by Vahuka for the ride to Kundina. 'What is this! Why have you chosen such lean and mean looking horses, Vahuka?' he seethed with anger. 'Why, they look hardly fit enough to make the trip to Kundina leave alone getting us there speedily! And you have promised to make the trip in a day!'

Vahuka was taken aback. He had used all his knowledge of horses to choose the very best steeds that he knew would run like the wind. He had whispered into the ears of each of the four horses words that he only knew, which would make them obey every subtle pull and tug at the reins he would be holding in his hands. But he bowed his head and said, 'Your Majesty, if you are not happy with my choice of horses, then point to me the horses you wish me to yoke to the chariot and I shall do as you wish.'

'No, no... I did not mean that, Vahuka,' Rituparna said. 'Your knowledge of horses far excels my own. It is just that in my eagerness to reach Kundina I have become impatient. I do not want to arrive late for Damayanti's swayamvara. I am sorry to have sounded mistrusting, because I have seen you have a magical way with horses and so place my full faith in your judgement. Harness the horses of your choice and let us be on our way!'

Vahuka turned to Varshaneya and instructed him on the positioning of the horses as each one was yoked to the chariot. Then he anointed the forehead of each horse with a vermilion mark while uttering a prayer. A quiver ran through each horse and the animal stiffened, stretched, and arched its neck in readiness.

'Climb on to the chariot, Your Highness,' Vahuka said, offering his hand. Then he climbed in alongside Varshaneya to whom he said, 'Pick up the reins and pull them taut the way I have taught, for you will drive the chariot for the first hundred *yojanas*[1], after which I shall take over the reins.'

When Vahuka noticed that Varshaneya was tiring, he took

[1] A yojana is a Vedic measure of distance that was used in ancient India. One yojana is about 12–15 km.

over the reins and flicked his whip over the horses' flanks being careful not to touch their skin. Just the sound of it made the horses leap forward and Rituparna felt a sudden forward jolt. Now it seemed to him as if the chariot almost flew into the air and the horses sped forward so fast that one couldn't even hear the sound of their hooves pounding the ground.

But it was this that set Varshaneya's mind racing in a different direction. So far, he had only picked up a few tips from Vahuka while grooming and exercising the horses around the stables. But this was something different altogether. He had only heard tales of Matali, the charioteer of Indra, who could drive like no other. Or of Salihotra who communicated with horses in mysterious ways and was well-versed in the technique of racing horses like no one else could. Had they taken shape in Vahuka, he wondered? Who else had he heard could drive a chariot like them? Then it struck him! *Aaahhh... yes, he had heard the fame of one Prince Nal of Vidarbha. Could this possibly be Nal? But no, although they would be about the same age, Nal was a handsome prince and here was a misshapen dwarf-like figure driving a chariot that surpassed anything he had heard!* Varshaneya scratched his head. *No, it's not possible... this has to be Vahuka only.*

On the other hand, Rituparna was equally amazed at the way the chariot seem to be now flying towards Kundina under the wondrous hands of Vahuka. His spirits soared as he now was assured that they would surely arrive well in time for Damayanti's swayamvara. But the lightning speed at which the horses were moving was creating such a strong current of wind that Rituparna's upper garment flew up and over his head and he was now bare-chested. 'Stop-stop the chariot! We must retrieve my garment that has flown away!' he shouted to Vahuka.

'We cannot stop now, my Lord!' shouted back Vahuka. 'It lies somewhere 15 yojanas behind. Even if we go back, we may never find it and will lose precious time!'

As the chariot sped on, Rituparna from a distance, glimpsed, a Vibhitaka tree laden with fruits. Using his skills in mathematics and calculations, he, counted in a flash how many fruits the tree bore on its boughs. Wanting to upstage Vahuka with his skill at horses and as a charioteer, he shouted out, 'Vahuka, I will prove my proficiency in calculation by telling you how many fruits hang on the branches of that Vibhitaka tree that you can see coming up. I judge that the leaves and fruits lying on the ground exceed those that are on it by 101. Now, according to me there are 50 million leaves on its two branches and 2095 fruits! What say you?'

Vahuka was nonplussed but he also knew the King was trying to be one up on him. 'Your Majesty, I wouldn't like to speculate. I will hew down the tree and then in your presence will count the leaves and fruits lying on the ground.'

'But we have no time to lose! I don't want to be late for the swayamvara! We cannot stop and wait for you to cut down the tree!'

'Your Highness, Kundina is not too far away now. From here on, the road lies straight ahead, so let Varshaneya take over the reins and you go on ahead.' suggested Vahuka.

'No! Definitely not!' said the king 'I won't risk the horses in Varshaneya's hands. They only understand your grip on their reins!'

'Then let us stop awhile. Let me count the leaves and fruits. And I promise I will still make up for the lost time and get you to Kundina well in time!' assured Vahuka. He got down from the chariot, withdrew the axe that was encased along its side, and felled the tree in quick strokes. He was amazed that the king's mental count of fruits tallied exactly as per his physical count. He turned to Rituparna and remarked, 'Your Majesty, I would be grateful if you would share your knowledge of calculation with me.' To which Rituparna, said, 'And Vahuka, you also know that there is no one more well-versed in the art and science of the dice game than me, as you have seen over the many games we have played out together.'

Vahuka pleaded, 'Yes, but if you impart all your knowledge of the dice, without holding anything back to me, I will in exchange share my secret knowledge of horses with you, Your Majesty.'

'So be it, Vahuka. I shall do so gladly.'

As soon as Rituparna telepathically imparted his secret knowledge of the dice, Vahuka immediately felt like vomiting and along with the virulent poison of Karkotaka, he also spewed out Kali who had been invading his body ever since that unfortunate day when he, as Nal, without purifying himself, had entered to offer the evening prayers and thus opened a gateway into his body through which Kali had taken possession of him.

Kali, invisible to both Rituparna and Varshaneya, fearing that he was about to face the wrath of Nal, fell down on his knees with folded hands begging him stay his anger. He pleaded that he too had lived a hellish life day and night, consumed by the fiery, venomous poison of the serpent Karkotaka who had bitten Nal. He promised Nal, that those who, in times to come, would recite the story of Nal, would be unaffected and remain free of the fear of the demonic powers of Kali. When he saw Nal's wrath subsiding but still fearing the worst, Kali immediately entered into the Vibhitaka tree. Ever since that day, this tree fell into disrepute as being possessed by the evil Kali.

With Kali out of his system, Vahuka felt more like himself although he still retained his misshapen, dwarf-like form. The entire episode had barely taken minutes, and soon Vahuka was back in the chariot urging the steeds towards Kundina... and Damayanti.

Chapter 25

Rituparna And Vahuka In Kundina

The sky thundered, the earth seemed to quake as the sound of a chariot's wheels and the thudding of sixteen hooves resounded around Kundina. People rushed out of their homes and those who were out in the streets froze in their tracks. Some pointed skywards while others looked towards the mountains to determine the direction from which the sounds were coming. Then someone spotted a speck in the distance that seemed to be moving rapidly towards the city. It quickly grew bigger and bigger until someone in the crowd spotted the flag of Ayodhya fluttering atop the chariot. The news spread rapidly and a messenger ran from the watch tower towards the palace to inform King Bhima that the King of Ayodhya was coming to their city.

Bhima was nonplussed. He had no prior knowledge of what Damayanti had planned and put into action, and therefore no intimation that a royal visit from Ayodhya was to be expected. So, he wondered what could possibly be the purpose of King Rituparna's visit. Damayanti, who was on her terrace, also heard the deafening rattle of chariot wheels and thundering hooves of horses being ridden towards Kundina and her heart began pounding in expectation. She knew only one man who could drive a chariot so fast and that man was Nal. The chariot, as it came into view, appeared to be moving on a cushion of air with the horses' hooves barely skimming the ground. The tall, imposing figure of a royal personage loomed over a dwarf-like figure who was driving the chariot. She saw the chariot roll to a halt. Varshaneya got down and held out his hand to help the king alight and then it was driven off by that dwarf-like charioteer towards the stables. But there was no sight of Nal although she could have sworn that she had expected him as the charioteer of Rituparna. Crestfallen, she walked towards her chamber.

By this time, Bhima had hastily arranged a reception committee to be present at the steps of the palace to welcome King Rituparna with garlands and a guard of honour.

'Welcome King Rituparna,' Bhima smiled graciously as he embraced the king. 'To what do we owe the honour of your gracious presence in our humble city?'

'I have been visiting some friendly neighbours King Bhima, and I could not go back to Ayodhya without seeing you.' Rituparna replied as his gaze quickly took in the fact that there were no brahmin priests, no sign of any other kings, no decorations indicating that a swayamvara was to take place. 'But, where are your sons, King Bhima? I do not see them here.'

'Oh, they are out on a hunt and should be back by the evening,' Bhima replied. 'But come, you must be tired and desire a rest after your long journey.' Turning to a royal guard, he said, 'Mahendra, please escort the King and his companion to the guest chambers.' Then turning to Rituparna, he said, 'We shall talk and dine together after you have rested. My sons and daughter Damayanti will be honoured to meet you.'

Damayanti beat her fist into her palm as she paced to and fro in her chamber. 'How can this be?' she muttered to herself. 'No one other than Nal could cover that distance between

Ayodhya and Kundina in such little time. Had Rituparna learnt the skill from Nal and it was him that rode the chariot here?' she asked her reflection in the mirror. *No, no... I don't think it could be that... besides Nal is the unbeaten champion in racing chariots!* 'Then who else could it be?' she asked her mirror image. 'Surely not that squat, ugly dwarf! He was obviously just a groom for the horses! Oh! This is maddening! Somehow I must find out more about him,' she decided.

Sending for the handmaiden she could trust, she told her, 'Kesinia, go seek out the charioteer of King Rituparna. Approach him respectfully and, regardless of his appearance, speak to him courteously. Find out whatever you can about him. Remember the tale Parnada told us when he returned from Ayodhya about this charioteer? Repeat the words of Parnada to him, and observe very carefully what this dwarf's reaction is when he hears your words. Somehow I have a feeling this could be Nal, although his appearance completely belies it. But don't say anything about my suspicions to him.'

'Don't you worry, Princess,' Kesinia said. 'I shall observe his every expression, memorise every word he utters.'

When she met the charioteer Vahuka, Kesinia said, 'Welcome to Kundina, noble charioteer! Our Princess Damayanti has sent me to enquire if you are comfortably settled in and whether there is anything lacking in our hospitality to our guests?'

'Your Princess is most gracious,' he answered.

'She also desires to know when you set out for Kundina and about the purpose of your visit,' Kesinia asked giving him her most beguiling smile.

'Our King had heard from a visiting brahmin that a second swayamvara was being held for Princess Damayanti, and he was eager to win her hand in marriage. We left Ayodhya yesterday and have arrived a while ago as you know. My horses are fleet-footed and I know how to speak to them. Thus they heed my commands and are capable of covering great distances in far less time than it would take ordinary horses to cover.'

'And who is the third person accompanying King Rituparna and yourself?' Kesinia probed, gently driving him into a conversation with her.

'He is Varshaneya, who I have learnt was once the charioteer of King Nal of Vidarbha,' replied Vahuka. When Nal had to leave his kingdom, his wife Damayanti had told Varshaneya to take their children to her father's place in Kundina and leave them there. On his return, Nal told him to go to King Rituparna in Ayodhya who was in need of a good charioteer so he had gone and found employment in Ayodhya.'

'But then surely Varshaneya would know the whereabouts of King Nal, where he went or where he is now?' queried Kesinia.

'No, Varshaneya has no clue to King Nal's whereabouts. He is probably wandering around, wherever he is in some kind of disguise to conceal his real identity. Only Nal himself would know where Nal is now,' Vahuka said in a tired voice and shrugged his shoulders.

Then Kesinia played the trump card, Damayanti had asked her to. She said, 'The Princess wishes to hear from your lips the exact words you said to Parnada when he met you in Ayodhya.'

Nal's heart overflowed with grief as he recited: 'A virtuous lady should not be angry with one that was deprived by birds of his garment while trying to procure food, and who is not burning in misery. Whether treated well or ill, she would never be angry seeing her husband in that plight, despoiled of his kingdom, bereft of prosperity, oppressed by hunger and overwhelmed with calamity.' While reciting this, Vahuka was overcome and tears began to flow from his eyes.

Seeing this, Kesinia bid him a kind farewell and returned to the palace where she reported to Damayanti the conversation she had with the charioteer Vahuka, and the effect it had on him. Now, Damayanti's heart told her that it was Vahuka who must be Nal. But still she needed more proof and so she now instructed Kesinia to be around Vahuka and observe him. If he were to ask her to fetch water or something to kindle a fire, she should delay getting it as far as she could. Meanwhile if she happened to see him perform any uncommon or superhuman act on his part, she was to report it immediately to her in full detail.

As she was going to engage Vahuka again in conversation, Kesinia saw him approaching through a low-rise doorway. Undeterred, Vahuka did not lower his head. Instead, he walked head held high and to Kesinia's amazement, the portal expanded and rose to its full height and the charioteer walked proudly through it. She followed him discreetly at a distance as he walked towards the kitchens. Once there, he checked the vegetables and meats laid out for being cooked. The fires were cold and there was no one in sight. Meanwhile, he knew Rituparna would be craving for some homemade food that Vahuka would supervise in the kitchens of Ayodhya.

Recalling the boon of Agni, he grabbed a handful of dried grass that was lying in a corner and held it up in both his hands towards the sun. Kesinia gasped as a ball of fire appeared and the grass was alight in Vahuka's hand. What's more, the fire didn't appear to singe his hand! What appeared magical to Kesinia didn't stop there. The fires lit and the food was now cooking on firewood; she then saw him take hold of a miserable looking bunch of withered herbs and rub them in both his palms. When he opened his palms, the herbs looked as if they had just been freshly picked! Their fragrance rose in the air as he chopped them and stirred them into the simmering pots.

She came rushing back to Damayanti, and with eyes nearly popping out of her head narrated all the wonders she had just witnessed Vahuka perform. Damayanti quickly issued further instructions: 'Go back again Kesinia and somehow bring back small portions the food that he has cooked and of which there must be still some left in the pots. Go quickly!'

When she saw Vahuka carrying some food out of the kitchen towards Rituparna's chamber, Kesinia stole into the kitchen and hurriedly scooped some food, which was still simmering over a very low fire now, into bowls lying there. She then covered them with a piece of cloth and hurried back. As soon as Damayanti had lifted the cloth, the aroma of the spices filled the air and she delicately plucked some vegetables from the pots and popped them into her mouth.

'This is he! It is him! The charioteer Vahuka is my Nal!' she cried, thrilled at her discovery.

Then suddenly, an inspiration struck her! She told Kesinia to collect the twins Indrasen and Indraseni. When they came, she cooed to them: 'Children, I want you to meet the greatest charioteer in the land, who is luckily visiting us at the moment.' Then turning to Kesinia, she said, 'Take them with you. Pretend that you are casually passing by the kitchens and make sure they meet Vahuka!'

As soon as he saw Kesinia approaching with the kids, Vahuka could not restrain himself and rushed forward to gather them in his embrace. Turning to Kesinia, who was gaping with her mouth open, he told her that he was reminded of his own twin children he had left behind in Nishadha.

'I understand how you feel Vahuka,' Kesinia said. 'It's natural to miss your children when you are far away from them.'

'Why are you crying, little man?' Indraseni asked in all innocence.

'Go now, Kesinia,' he said, brushing away his tears with the sleeve of his garment. 'Take them back to their mother.'

Chapter 26

The Reunion

When Kesinia came back with the twins, they rushed to their mother who held them both in her embrace.

'Mother!' exclaimed Indrasen. 'That dwarf hugged me so tight!'

'And he kissed my forehead and hugged me too!' said a delighted Indraseni.

Over their heads, Damayanti looked enquiringly at Kesinia who nodded her head in agreement.

'That's was so nice of him, children,' Damayanti told them. 'Now go and play while I talk to Kesinia.'

After Kesinia told Damayanti how the charioteer had got so emotionally worked up upon seeing the children, there was barely any doubt left in her mind that Vahuka was her husband Nal. But one unexplained fact remained, the thought of which nagged her: *How could Nal have possibly transformed into this misshapen dwarf-like figure?* Putting that thought aside, she told Kesinia to go and tell her mother that she wanted to meet her.

'Mother…' Damayanti said, and burst into tears.

'Now-now, what is this… what has happened Damayanti?' her mother said holding her in a warm embrace. 'Stop crying my child, and tell me what is bothering you.'

'You know I have been telling you of my suspicions about that charioteer whose name is Vahuka,' began Damayanti. 'Well, I have secretly carried out many tests to discover his identity and now I have no doubt whatsoever that he is my husband Nal.'

'I think it is high time now that we told your father about all this,' remarked her mother. 'We have kept him completely in the dark up till now and that is not right.'

'Yes, I agree with you Mother.'

The next day, Damayanti asked her mother, 'Has Father agreed to let me proceed as I see fit?'

'Yes, he has my dear daughter. He too wants to see you reunited with your husband.'

Then give me your permission to call Vahuka here and I will confront him. It's time we resolved this issue now… the suspense has been fraying my nerves ever since he came here. I cannot bear it any longer!'

The Queen Mother turned to Kesinia and said, 'Go tell the charioteer Vahuka that the Queen Mother wishes to meet him, and bring him back with you here.'

When Vahuka appeared, he was surprised to see Damayanti clad in a simple red garment and her hair all loose, looking as if she hadn't slept in a long, long while. However, after the first quick glance he kept his head bowed not being able to bear the pained look in her eyes.

'Vahuka,' Damayanti said. 'Have you come across a noble man who abandoned his beloved and blameless wife in a forest while she was sleeping? Why did he, whom I chose as my husband in preference to the four gods… what made him, the father of my two children, leave me alone at the mercy of robbers and highwaymen? Did he not stop to think that I could have fallen into their hands and lost my honour?'

Tears had begun streaming from her eyes and Vahuka unable to control himself said, 'Neither the loss of my kingdom, nor my act of deserting you was of my own free will. Both these despicable acts were performed by Kali who had entered my body and subverted my mind by taking possession of me.

When you silently cursed him in the woods, he continued to dwell in my body. Do you remember, it was Kali who had loaded the dice and made me lose my kingdom and then everything along with it? This body that you see me in now was both a curse and a blessing from the serpent Karkotaka. He was the one who sent me to Rituparna, who seeing a misshapen, dwarf-like creature, would never recognise me as his old friend Nal but seeing my skill with horses, Karkotaka assured me that Rituparna would hire me as his charioteer.'

'Oh Nal, what miseries you have had to endure over these years…' lamented Damayanti, her tears now copiously flowing down her cheeks. 'But how did Kali finally leave your body?'

'He was forced to actually,' Nal replied. 'When Rituparna had passed on his skill at the dice, which is unmatched and far superior to anyone's on earth or heaven, Kali was repelled. Along with the poison of Karkotaka in my body which had been consuming him all this time, he was in such pain that he was forcefully evicted when I vomited the poison from my entrails. He then begged my forgiveness and disappeared into the trunk of a tree.'

'That demon Kali ruined everything for us… and above everything else, also separated us,' Damayanti flared up. 'I pity the poor people he will now keep tormenting!'

'What tormented me most was when I heard the news of your second swayamvara!' Nal said, the anguish on his face plain to see. 'How could you even think of a second husband, Damayanti? After all the vows we exchanged to never part from each other, had you in your despair and anger decided to cast all that aside and move on with your life?'

Damayanti heard Nal's recriminations is silence, and simply said, 'You were the one who left.'

Ignoring that, Nal continued, 'When I heard Rituparna say he wanted to win your hand in marriage, can you even imagine the hell I went through?'

'It was a ruse I was compelled to adopt to get you here from wherever you were hiding, Nal!' she cried. 'Believe me, the thought of any other man has not ever crossed my mind. How can it, Nal! I am the mother of your two children! Let the gods who blessed our wedding strike me dead here and now, should I be found lacking in my vows as a wife!'

Her plaint rose to the heavens, and the sky rumbled as Varuna declared: 'She has done no wrong, Nal! Well-preserving the honour of her family as well as yours, Damayanti has stayed true to you through all the trials and tribulations you put her through by your act of desertion. I would even say that she has not only upheld but also enhanced the honour of both the royal houses, in fact, both the kingdoms of Vidarbha and Nishadha!' Likewise, Agni, Yama and Indra also echoed the sentiments expressed by Varuna, god of wind, and praised the virtuous Damayanti's high moral standing among all women. 'She,' they said, 'would stand as a beacon of wifely forbearance and devotion for future generations to come in all the yugas.'

'The failing has been yours, Nal. She and her children are the ones who had to suffer ignominy and untold grief through your fondness for the game of dice,' the gods said. 'A worthier wife you will never find. Embrace her as your *ardhangini*, your better half, and live happily ever after.'

Nal bowed his head in acceptance. Then he suddenly remembered the gift of Karkotaka he had been carrying in a bundle under his arm. He took the translucent white robe from it and with a graceful gesture wrapped it around his shoulders. As soon as it was draped on him, it emanated a dazzling, blinding flash of white light. Damayanti shut her eyes against the glare and when it subsided, Nal stood transformed before her in all his former stature and beauty.

Karkotaka had been as good as his word. Nal blinked and stared down at himself, hardly believing his own eyes. He ran his hands over his face, his arms, his thighs, witnessing the transformation that had taken place. Then he took two steps towards Damayanti and embraced her in the warmth of his strong arms. He bent his mouth to her ear and whispered, 'Forgive me?'

She looked up at him and smiled. 'There is nothing to forgive. Our love has been tested by the fires of misfortune, but has endured and emerged purer, stronger and more precious than ever before. Come, husband… let us now go meet my parents and our children. They have missed you so!'

King Bhima was overjoyed at the return of his son-in-law Nal. The glow on his daughter's face had returned and the children Indrasen and Indraseni were beside themselves with joy at having their father back with them.

Rituparna was grace personified. When he realised that Vahuka was, in fact, Nal, his long-time friend, he embraced him warmly and sought his forgiveness for any act of discourtesy he may have committed during Nal's stay with him while he was disguised as the dwarf Vahuka. In return, Nal sought his friend's forgiveness for the deception he had been compelled to play on him on the advice of Karkotaka.

'All's well that ends well,' King Bhima patted Nal on his back.

'Yes… but all is not over yet,' murmured Nal.

Chapter 27

The Second Game Of Dice

Nal and Damayanti spent a pleasant month of togetherness to make up for all the lost time when they were apart; a month in which Nal regained all his physical strength and balance of mind. It was now time to plan his future course of action and in this he took King Bhima's sage advice. Together, they devised a strategy to win back his kingdom and re-establish him as the rightful monarch of Nishadha.

On an auspicious day divined by the court astrologers of King Bhima, Nal, garlanded by Damayanti, set out for Giriprastha in regal splendour. Ahead of his gem-studded, golden chariot drawn by four magnificent steeds marched a richly-liveried bodyguard. Driving the chariot was his trusted charioteer Varshaneya behind which rode fifty armed horsemen, sixteen richly-caparisoned elephants, and six hundred infantrymen.

News of his impending arrival at Giriprastha preceded Nal's arrival. Vasumati, was overjoyed at the prospect of being reunited with her elder son in whose banishement she had secretly wept and wilted during all these years, but had not had the will nor the moral standing to overrule her young son Pushkar's decree. She wondered what hand Fate would deal now that Nal was, in all likelihood, returning to Giriprastha with some plan to confront Pushkar who had through devious means connived at his banishment.

When it reached the ears of his brother Pushkar, he wondered what Nal could possibly want with him after all these years. 'Let him come… we shall see what he now has on mind,' he thought, rubbing his hands in unholy glee.

As Nal was escorted into his brother, King Pushkar's presence, Pushkar, feigning delight, stepped forward and greeted his brother with a broad smile which bordered on a smirk.

'Welcome brother, how very nice to see you again after all these years!' Pushkar said grasping Nal by both his shoulders. 'And to what do I owe the pleasure of this visit? I last remember seeing you and your wife in peasants' garments when I banished you both from the kingdom.'

Nal did not fail to note the sarcasm and the intense dislike that lurked behind Pushkar's greeting. But controlling his own pent-up rage, he told his brother that good fortune had favoured him, as Pushkar could no doubt see, from the elephants and army that accompanied him on this visit.

'Well, well… I am happy to see you are still alive and that the gods have out of pity seen fit to smile on you at last. And how is my sister-in-law Damayanti, still as ravishingly beautiful as she once was?' Pushkar's words twisted the knife reminding Nal of his shameful banishment.

'All is as it should be, Pushkar,' Nal coolly replied. 'What I have really come here for is to challenge you again in a game of dice. And you know, as well as I, that dharma, self-honour, and principle decree that you accept the challenge by which, with God's grace, I can win back all that I lost to you.'

'Hmmmm…. You are right in the matter of dharma and self-honour,' Pushkar mused rubbing his chin. 'But then, you also know I am not particularly dharmic. As for God's grace, well… I am not too sure about that! Besides, have you forgotten that I have the Devil's luck in dice? I have no further wish to disgrace you and send you packing again into the wilderness. As for your elephants and army, and that miserable bodyguard, I am neither impressed nor have any need of them.'

Inwardly enraged but outwardly retaining his composure,

Nal replied, 'If you refuse my challenge at dice, Pushkar, then I will have to resort to the option of inviting you to single combat with the choice of your weapon. Should I lose, well you can do what you like... behead me if you want. But, should I win, it will be you who will have to go into exile.'

'Well brother, I am happy at your immense good fortune and that you are also a fool enough to stake it all over again in a game of dice. I am also rather surprised to hear that the beauteous Damayanti is still with you and hasn't left a beleaguered man like you in your days of misfortune. What wouldn't I do to have such a wife!' Pushkar jeered.

'Well here is your chance then, brother. This time I stake Damayanti as well. Should you win, you can have your wish!' Nal offered, although he was seething with anger at Pushkar's comment.

'Done!' Pushkar laughed. Then turning to his personal attendant, he threw him a key and said: 'Bring out the chausar and the dice from that's locked in my cupboard!'

'Come, brother, let us play!' Pushkar. 'Since I won the first time, I get to roll the dice first.'

'Go right ahead, brother,' Nal conceded.

At the back of his mind, Pushkar still felt the dice retained their original power that Kali had invested them with because he had never again felt the need to use those particular set of dice in a game. So, with an exaggerated gesture of rolling the dice in his palms, he flung them on the chausar. And as they fell, his popped wide open and a gasp escaped his lips. It was a two – the worst throw he had made in his life!

Nal kept a straight face and appeared to be doing some calculation on his fingers.

'What on earth are you counting!' exclaimed a highly irritated Pushkar.

Closing his eyes and drawing in a deep breath, Nal rolled the dice in his palm. Then at the appropriate count, he opened his palm and let the dice roll. It was a six, the best throw of the dice! In that one throw, Nal had won back everything – his throne, his kingdom, his palace, his elephants, his armies – everything!

The blood drained from Pushkar's face and he felt dizzy and faint. Nal summoned a handmaiden and asked her to fetch a bowl of water, which he sprinkled on his brother's face to revive him.

A flustered Pushkar shook his head to come to his senses and then he fell at Nal's feet. 'Forgive me Nal, I am after all your younger brother and we are family,' he pleaded.

'You have been a wretched king and, moreover, a shameless man Pushkar. Even if I forget and forgive your pact with the demon Dwapara and that evil Kali to disinherit me, I can never overlook your despicable act of casting covetous, lustful eyes on your own sister-in-law Damayanti. For that act alone I would have you blinded you fool. But no, I am not a vengeful man,' Nal said. 'We are after all related by blood. What's more, I know that your foul victory at the first game of dice was not really your intention – that demon Dwapara had perverted your mind and Kali did all the rest by ensuring your victory in the game of dice. I cannot in all truth lay their diabolic acts on your head.'

'So, you are not going to have me imprisoned for life?' blabbered a relieved Pushkar.

'Get up brother,' Nal said offering his hand to raise Pushkar from the floor. 'I not only grant you your life, but also your rightful share in the kingdom of our forebears. I still love you, as I always have, as my younger brother. Go, return to your former kingdom in the east of our region and rule there wisely and live happily with your family. You will always be welcome to come and visit us any time you wish.'

Over the next few days, Nal sent a royal entourage to bring King Bhima, Queen Charumati and Damayanti along with her twins and her brothers to Giriprastha. After the ceremonies of reinstating Nal to the throne were completed, King Bhima came to Giriprastha laden with gifts from his son-in-law. With Nal restored to the throne of Giriprastha, all the brahmins, the courtiers and the people of the city rejoiced. Law and order once again prevailed in the kingdom and everyone was at peace.

One evening, in the privacy of their bedchamber, Damayanti playfully brought out the chausar.

'How about one game of dice between us, dear husband?' she asked with a beguiling smile.

'What do you want to stake?' Nal teased. 'Roll it up and lock it away. I am all yours... now and forever.'

APPENDIX

Legends surrounding Nal

The romance of Nal and Damayanti, because it appears in several different versions in Bengali, Telegu, Tamil, Malayalam, and in the legend of *Dhola Maru* of Rajasthani folklore, is surrounded by several variations and interpolations in its telling. The more interesting of these pertain to Nal's past loves and how they played a role in his final and abiding marriage to Damayanti, the daughter of King Bhima of Vidarbha.

Nal's previous lives

In a previous life, Nal had met the daughter of the Naga Vasuki – Lord Shiva's snake who lay coiled around His neck. He was also the King of all serpents and had a gem called *Nagamani* on his head. When the gods and *asuras* (demons) performed the *samudra manthan* (churning of the ocean of milk) to gain *amrit* (nectar of life), Shiva gave them Vasuki to use as a long, thick and strong rope to wind around Mount Mandara with which they could do the churning.

Upon seeing Nal, Vasuki's daughter fell instantly in love and wished to marry him. But since Nal, because of his close friendship with Vasuki, regarded her like a daughter, he told her that he could marry her only if she would be reborn again as a human. After some years, she was reborn as a human princess named Damayanti. When she became of age, her father sent an invitation to Indra to come to her swayamvara but the swan carrying the invitation fell into Nal's hands instead. Damayanti's father, King Bhima, then sent a second invitation to Indra. Thus, both Nal and Indra arrived to claim Damayanti's hand in marriage. Because Nal was human, Damayanti was able to identify him despite the tricks employed by Indra.

Nal and the goddess Motini

Another legend surrounding Nal is that of the goddess Motini. When Nal's mother was pregnant and carrying him in her womb, the co-wives of King Virasena plotted against her and convinced the king that the child, if born, would be the death of his father. With deep regret and sorrow, King Virasena sent an assassin to kill the Queen but the man killed a doe instead, and took back the doe's eyes to prove that the Queen was dead along with the child in her womb. When her time came, the Queen gave birth to Nal and a compassionate merchant adopted her as his daughter and raised Nal as his grandson.

When he grew into a young, handsome man, the goddess Motini fell in love with him. But she was apprehensive of his caste when he mentioned that he was a merchant. So she invited him to play the game of dice in order to discover his real identity. At first Nal declined to play saying that it was a game only for those who wear turbans – meaning kings. But when he won, it was evident to her that he must be of royal blood.

Madly in love, Motini and Nal got married, but she later told him that she would only bring him unhappiness. 'I am the daughter of a goddess,' she said. 'Your kingdom will perish because I cannot carry a child in my womb. If you marry a human, you will have children and your throne will be secured and your dynasty will flourish.'

Motini then went to the court of Nal's father, King Virasena, who fell in love with her but she refused to marry anyone unless the *Nal Katha* (story of Nal) was told.

The magical flowers

Vasuki's daughter had given Nal a flower that transformed into a 100-year old man. Thus transformed, Nal had said, 'Oh! I don't think that I will be recognised by my love... She will say, 'Where has this half-dead, old man come from? She will kill me!' Vasuki's daughter then gave him a second flower that would restore him to his youthful, handsome form and told him to keep both the flowers.

Now Nal, as an old man, came to his father King Virasena's court and narrated the Nal Katha (his own life story up to that point). Everyone at the court recognised that the old man actually was Nal and reunited him with his wife Motini. The King also sent for his Queen, Nal's mother. On smelling the second flower, Nal was restored his former youth and good looks. But because Motini could not bear children due to her non-human birth, she left for Indra's *swargalok* (heaven), so that Nal could marry again.

After this, Nal married Damayanti at her swayamvara.

Notes

Chapter 1 – The mortal who rivalled the gods

The River Payoshini

The Payoshini was an ancient river, also known as the Purna, which the Vishnu Purana says was brought by Vayu and Kurma down to the plains from the Vindhyan mountain range. According to the Mahabharata, the Pandavas had visited this place as part of their pilgrimage. Yudhishthir, having bathed in this river, comes to the Vaidurya mountain and the River Narmada. With the geographical description mentioned in the Mahabharata, the present-day Tapti river is considered as the original Payoshini. The word 'purna' means 'complete' in Sanskrit, and River Purna was also called Payoshini or Paisani – both words whose meaning translates as 'Ambrosia'.

The Vindhya Mountains

The Vindhyas are of significance in Indian mythology and history. Several ancient texts mention the Vindhyas as the southern boundary of Aryavarta, territorial region of the ancient Indo-Aryan peoples. Although today Indo-Aryan languages are spoken south of the Vindhyas, the range continues to be considered as the traditional boundary between north and south

India. This mountain range is a complex, discontinuous chain of mountain ridges, hill ranges, highlands and plateau escarpments in west-central India. The exact extent of the Vindhyas is generally defined and, historically, the term covered a number of distinct hill systems in central India, including the one that is now known as the Satpura Range. Today, the term principally refers to the escarpment that runs north of and roughly parallel to the Narmada River in Madhya Pradesh, and its hilly extensions. Depending on the definition, the range extends up to Gujarat in the west, and Uttar Pradesh and Bihar in the east. In certain Puranas, the term Vindhya specifically covers the mountain range located between the Narmada and the Tapti rivers; that is, the one which is now known as the Satpura Range. The Varaha Purana uses the name *Vindhya-pada* (foot of the Vindhyas) for the Satpura range.

The Riksha Mountains

The *Nalopakhyan* episode in the Vana Parva of the Mahabharata places the Riksa Mountain between Avanti and Daksinapatha. Thus the mountain, when referred to incidentally in literature, is invariably associated with the middle Narmada region. Mahismati was the most important city, and the Dasarna – a notable river and the mountain lay in Sagar, a region of the central Vindhyas.

Rising from the Riksha mountains ranged along the northern borders of Vidarbha, the Payoshini river entered the dark and deep Dandaka Forest and flowed through it, nurturing the land as it wound its way through the kingdom ruled by the heroic King Bhima of the Bhoja Yadava lineage.

The Kingdom of Bhima

While the kingdom lying south of the Vindhya range prospered as a result of the river Payoshini's bounty, the womb of King Bhima's wife continued to remain barren through the years. Ancient scriptures describe the Dandaka forest, bordered on two sides by the Godavari and Narmada rivers, as a rampant wilderness – its tree cover so thick that the rays of the sun could barely penetrate through the dense foliage. Valmiki, while writing his epic poem Ramayana, describes it as "a wilderness over which several hermitages are scattered, while wild beasts and asuras everywhere abound." This was the forest that was 'home' to Ram, Sita and Lakshman where they spent thirteen years of their exile, far from their kingdom of Ayodhya in the north.

Chapter 3 – She who walks in beauty

Characteristics of Damayanti

Damayanti has been compared to 'lightning' twice – once in the Vana Parva of the Mahabharata (Chapter 53.10-14), and again at the time of her entry into Suktimati, the capital city of Chedi – 'you dazzle like lightning in the midst of clouds'. Girls who bear this name are excellent at analysing, understanding, and learning. They tend to be mystics, philosophers, scholars, or teachers. Because they live so much in the mind, they tend to be quiet and introspective, and are usually introverts. When presented with issues, they will see the larger picture. Their solitary thoughtfulness and analysis of people and world events may make them appear aloof, or sometimes even melancholy.

Chapter 4 – A Bevy of Swans

Symbolism of the Swan in Hinduism

The *Hansa*, or the Swan, is the symbol of Brahman-Atman in Hindu iconography and is often identified with the Supreme Spirit, Ultimate Reality, or Brahman. The flight of the Hansa symbolises *moksha* – the release from the cycle of *samsara* (endless cycle of birth-death-rebirth). Lake Manasarovar in Hindu mythology is regarded as the summer abode of the Hansa. The *Arayanna* or heavenly Hansas often feature in Hindu mythology and also find mention in the Ramayana. They play a pivotal role in the story of Nal and Damayanti where they carry messages between the two lovers. Swans are said to feed on pearls and are capable of separating milk from water in a mixture of both.

Chapter 16 – The Die is Cast

The Dice:

The nuts of the Vibhitaka tree are rounded but with five flatter sides and were used as dice in the game of chausar. In the dice game between Nal and Pushkar, the demon Kali transformed himself into the principal dice to be cast at the game. A handful of nuts would be cast on a chausar made of cloth with four strips extending from its centre in the directions of north, south, east and west. The players would have to call whether an odd or even number of nuts had been thrown. In the Nalopakhyan, King Rituparna demonstrates his ability to count large numbers instantaneously by counting the number of nuts on an entire bough.

It appears that these nuts were also used as dice in the game between Yudhishthir and Duryodhana narrated in the Mahabharata epic. In the Virata Parva (Book 3), Yudhishthir carries 'black and red dice with gold inlay and inset with sapphires'. Ved Vyasa, the author of the epic, while describing the game of dice between Yudhishthir and Shakuni, speaks of Shakuni, a supremely gifted and skilled player and Dvapara-incarnate, cheating during the throw of dice.

Chapter 18 – At the Crossroad

The Yakshas

In Hinduism, Manibhadra is an avatar of Shiva when he was angry and summoned for warfare. Manibhadra decimated the army of Jalandhara along with Virabhadra, another avatar of Shiva. In the Mahabharata, Manibhadra is mentioned along with Kubera as a chief of the Yakshas. Kubera is sometimes mentioned as a Rakshasa king. Kubera ruled a Yaksha kingdom of enormous wealth.

The Ashoka Tree:

The Ashoka tree (Saraca asoca – lit., 'sorrow-less') belongs to the Caesalpinioideae sub-family and not only does it play an important tree in the cultural traditions of the Indian subcontinent and adjacent areas, it is also considered sacred in India, Nepal and Sri Lanka. This tree has many associations in religion, folklore, and literature of these regions. It was also valued for its handsome appearance – for the colour and abundance of its flowers. It was often found in royal palace compounds and gardens, as well as close to temples throughout India.

The Ashoka tree is worshipped during Chaitra. In lunar religious calendars, Chaitra begins with the new moon in March-April and is the first month of the year. The first day of Chaitra is celebrated as New Year's Day, known as Gudi Padwa in Maharashtra, Chaitrai Vishu or Puthandu in Tamil Nadu, and Ugadi in Karnataka and Andhra Pradesh.

The Ashoka tree is also associated with Kamadeva, the Hindu god of love, who included an Ashoka blossom among the five flowers in his quiver, in which the Ashoka flower represents seductive hypnosis. Hence, the Ashoka tree is often mentioned in classical Indian religious and amorous poetry, having at least 16 different names in Sanskrit, referring to the tree or its flowers – Ashoka, Sita-ashoka, Aganapriya, Ashopalava, Asupala, Apashaka, Hemapushpa, Kankeli, Madhupushpa, Pindapushpa, Pindipushpa, Vanjula, Vishoka and Vichitra.

In Mahākāvya, or Indian epic poetry, the Ashoka tree is mentioned in the Ramayana in reference to the Ashoka Vatika (garden of Ashoka trees) where Hanuman first meets Sita in the palace gardens of Ravana.

Chapter 19 – Venom Of Karkotaka

Karkotaka – the king of snakes

Karkotaka is one of the powerful snakes or Nagas in Hindu tradition with numerous magical powers. His parents were

Sage Kashyapa and Kadru. The most popular and important part played by Karkotaka in Hindu mythology is in the story of Nal and Damayanti. Legend has it that once Karkotaka had cheated Sage Narad and the angry sage cursed him saying that he would become immobile – he would not be able to move his body. The sage then predicted that he would be relieved of his curse by Nal. The descendants of Karkotaka Naga are today settled in Rajasthan and are known as Katewa. There are temples dedicated to Karkotaka in Rajasthan, where he is the patron deity of the Katewa community. In Chikhaldara in Maharashtra there is a hill named after Karkotaka and the hill also has a famous temple dedicated to Nag Karkotaka Maharaj.

Chapter 20 – Maid in Waiting

The kingdom of Chedi

The ancient kingdom of Chedi lay roughly in the Bundelkhand division of Madhya Pradesh to the south of the River Yamuna, and along the River Betwa or Vetravati. The Chedi clan or dynasty was founded by King Abhichandra whose son and successor was the well-known King Vasu. During the Mahabharata war, the Chedis were ruled by Shishupala, an ally of Jarasandha of Magadha and Duryodhana of Hastinapur. He was a rival of Vasudeva Krishna who was his uncle's son.

King Sudaman of Dasarna had two daughters. One of them, Charumati was married to King Bhima of Vidarbha, and the other daughter Sagarika, who was the maternal aunt of Damayanti, was married to the Chedi King Suvahu (Viravahu). Unknown to her, Damayanti seeks and finds refuge here.

In the medieval period, the southern frontiers of Chedi extended to the banks of the Narmada River. Sotthivatnagara, the Sukti or Suktimati (Sagar, Madhya Pradesh) mentioned in Mahabharata, was the capital of Chedi. The Chedi kingdom was one of many kingdoms ruled during early periods by the Paurava kings, and later by the Yaduvanshi Rajput kings in central and western India. The Chedis are also mentioned in the Rigveda.

One branch of the Chedis founded a royal dynasty in the kingdom of Kalinga, according to the Hathigumpha inscription at Kharvela.

Chapter 21 – The Stables of Ayodhya

The city of Ayodhya

Ayodhya, also known as Saket, is an ancient city of India on the right bank of the River Saryu, 8 km from present-day Faizabad. This town is closely associated with Rama, seventh incarnation of Vishnu. According to the Ramayana, the city is 9,000 years old and was founded by Manu, the first man (the first woman was Shatarupa) in the universe according to the Vedas. Other sources hold that it was founded by its namesake, King Ayudh. It was said to be the capital of the Suryavanshi (Solar) dynasty, of which Rama was the most celebrated king.

The Skanda Purana and other Puranas list Ayodhya as one of the seven most sacred cities of India, as it has been the backdrop for much of Hindu scripture. Today, it is predominantly a religious destination with its historical significance and sacred temples. The Atharvaveda described Ayodhya as 'a city built by God and being prosperous as paradise itself'.

Chapter 24 – Damayanti invites Rituparna

King Rituparna of Ayodhya

In the 'Nalopakhyan' (the episode of Nal-Damayanti in Chapter VII of the Mahabharata), King Rituparna, son of King Sarvakama, ruled over Ayodhya sometime around 4720 BCE. Nal, in disguise, entered into his service, sometime after losing his kingdom in the game of dice with his brother Pushkar. Rituparna was a master mathematician and skilled in the game of dice.

On the advice of Karkotaka, the king of snakes, Nal as Vahuka, found service as a charioteer, and later as a minister, in King Rituparna's court. Karkotaka told Nal that he could learn and master the skills at dice from the King, which he could then use to defeat Pushkar and regain his kingdom.

According to the story in the Mahabharata, after the disappearance of Nal, Damayanti and her father sent out a search party to find him. One of the courtiers reported a person 'resembling in behaviour, but not in features' with Nal in Rituparna's court in Ayodhya. To verify this report, it was proclaimed that Damayanti had assented to remarry and consequently an invitation to her second swayamvara was also sent to Rituparna.

Bibliography

Mahabharata of Krishna Dwaipayana Vyasa – Book 3: Nalopakhyana Parva (Sections: 52-79) of the Vana Parva (Book of the Forest), English translation by K. M. Ganguli

The Tale of Nala, an unfinished poem by Sri Aurobindo

Nala and Damayanti, (Books 1-26) a long poem by Reverend Henry Hart Milman

Nalodaya of Kavi Kalidas (Books 1-4) translated into English by W. Yates, D.D.

Naishdhiyacharit Mahakavyam, by Mahakavi Shri Harsh Praneet. Hindi translation and commentary by Mohandev Pant

Nala Damayanti, by Jayant Joglekar

Splitting the Difference – Gender and Myth in ancient Greece and India, Wendy Doniger

Nala – Wikipedia

Damayanti – Wikipedia

Nishadha Kingdoms – Wikipedia

The Culture and Civilisation of Ancient India, D. D. Kosambi

Some Ksatriya Tribes of Ancient India – Dr. Bimla Charan Law, P.hD, Fellow of Royal Historical Society, London

Early History of India, V.A. Smith

Hindus: Their Religious Beliefs and Practices, Julius Lipner

Dharma: Its Early History in Law, Religion and Narrative contributed by Alf Hiltebeitel

About the Author

An alumunus of St. Stephen's college, Delhi University, Shivdutt Sharma graduated with Honours in History and did his post-graduation in English Literature. Working as a senior Copywriter and subsequently as a Creative Director with several advertising agencies in Mumbai, he is now an Editor with a publishing firm. His earlier published works include books for children that impart moral values, a personal memoir of his early days in Mussoorie, titled *The Hill Billy*, and a mythological romance titled *The Triumph of Love* – the immortal tale of Savitri and Satyavan.

He presently resides in Mumbai.

The author may be contacted on email:
shivds@gmail.com

For further details, contact:
Yogi Impressions Books Pvt. Ltd.
1711, Centre 1, World Trade Centre,
Cuffe Parade, Mumbai 400 005, India.

Fill in the Mailing List form on our website and receive, via email, information on books, authors, events and more.
Visit: www.yogiimpressions.com

Telephone: (022) 61541500, 61541541
E-mail: yogi@yogiimpressions.com

TITLES BY SHIVDUTT SHARMA AVAILABLE FROM YOGI IMPRESSIONS

Mythology / Romance

Autobiography / Memoir

Children's Books

Available as E-book

Available as E-book

Available as E-book